The State in Relation to Labour

Classics in Economic Series

American Capitalism: The Concept of Countervailing Power
John Kenneth Galbraith
with a new introduction by the author

The Chicago School of Political Economy
Warren J. Samuels, editor

Economic Semantics, Fritz Machlup

Economics and the Good Life, Bertrand de Jouvenel
edited and with a new introduction by
Dennis Hale and Marc Landy

The Economics of Population: Key Classic Writing
Julian L. Simon

The Economics of Welfare, Arthur Cecil Pigou
with a new introduction by Nahid Aslanbeigui

Economists and the Economy: The Evolution of Economic Ideas
Roger F. Backhouse

Economists and the Public, Harold William Hutt

The Economy as a System of Power: Corporate Systems
Marc R. Tool and Warren J. Samuels, editors

Epistemics and Economics: A Critique of Economic Doctrines
G. L. S. Shackle

Essays: On Entrepreneurs, Innovations, Business Cycles, and the Evolution of Capitalism,
Joseph A. Schumpeter

The Ethic of Competition, Frank Hyneman Knight
with a new introduction by Richard Boyd

The Future of Economics, Alexander J. Field, editor

The Future of Industrial Man, Peter Drucker

History and Historians of Political Economy
Werner Stark, edited by Charles M. A. Clark

Institutional Economics volumes 1 & 2, John R. Commons

The State in Relation to Labour, W. Stanley Jevons
with a new introduction by Warren J. Samuels

with a new introduction by Warren J. Samuels

W. Stanley Jevons

The State in Relation to Labour

Routledge
Taylor & Francis Group
LONDON AND NEW YORK

Originally published in 1887 by Macmillan and Co.

Published 2002 by Transaction Publishers

Published 2017 by Routledge
2 Park Square, Milton Park, Abingdon, Oxon OX14 4RN
711 Third Avenue, New York, NY 10017, USA

Routledge is an imprint of the Taylor & Francis Group, an informa business

Library of Congress Catalog Number: 2001027311

Library of Congress Cataloging-in-Publication Data

Jevons, William Stanley, 1835-1882.
The state in relation to labour / W. Stanley Jevons; with a new introduction by Warren J. Samuels.
p.cm.—(Classics in economics series.)
Originally published: London; New York: Macmillan, 1887.
Includes bibliographical references.
ISBN 0-7658-0867-6 (pbk. : alk. paper)
1. Labor laws and legislation—Great Britain—History—19th century.
2. Labor movement—Great Britain—History—19th century. I. Title.
II. Classics in economics.

KD3009 .J48 2001
344.4101—dc21 2001027311

ISBN 13: 978-0-7658-0867-7 (pbk)

CONTENTS

INTRODUCTION TO THE TRANSACTION EDITION

WILLIAM Stanley Jevons (1835-1882) was one of the first great virtuoso scholars in economics—or in political economy, as it was then known. He was a great theorist: his *Theory of Political Economy* (1871) was a major work of economic theory and helped establish him as a leader in the then widely developing but not new approach of marginal utility economics. He combined theoretical, institutional, and historical analyses—in effect amplifying Malthusian population theory—in *The Coal Question* (1885), concluding that the future of this then-basic industry was bleak, and therefore so was the British economy that was so dependent on coal. He engaged in statistical analyses in a number of fields, perhaps most notably in the study of business cycles, in which he related periodicity to sunspot phenomena. He studied the institutions of money and credit in a manner that enriched monetary theory, e.g., *Money and the Mechanism of Exchange* (1875); (see also the edited volume, *Investigations in Currency and Finance* [1884]). He worked in epistemology and philosophy of science, authoring *Pure Logic, or the Logic of Quality apart from Quantity* (1863) and *The Principles of Science: A Treatise on Logic and Scientific Method* (1874). He examined the problems of social change in *Methods of Social Reform and Other Papers* (1883). And he tackled the great problem of Victorian Britain, "the social question," that of the position of labour and the relation of the state to labour—the book herein reissued—in a manner which combined historical, institutional, and theoretical acumen with a minimum of manifest ideological bias. It is difficult to find another economist of his period who wrote so deeply on so many different subjects, who deployed such a variety of investigational techniques, and who both understood and advanced our understanding of the epistemological limits of the varied works of science. For Jevons, it was only *pure* economic theory, not economics as a whole, that comprised the study of the mechanics of utility. He understood that economic phenomena and performance were institutionally and historically grounded, such that pure economic theory had to be applied, combined with other techniques of analysis, when economists came to the study of real-world arrangements and problems. He shared—and, more important, demonstrated—the view of his great English contemporary, Alfred Marshall, that economics was an engine of inquiry, a set of tools with which one studied the economy, not a definition of economic reality itself.

Thus, the entry on "Jevons as an Economic Theorist" in *The New Palgrave* correctly identifies the areas of his theoretical contributions: (1) Mathematics, Utilitarianism and Methodology, (2) The Theory of Exchange, (3) The Theory of Labour and Exchange-with-Production, (4) The Theory of Rent, (5) The Theory of Capital and Interest, and (6) Distribution and Value: Further Considerations. But, as the foregoing paragraph indicates, Jevons was much more than a pure theorist. He was a political economist, an economic sociologist, in short, someone who understood that logic and empiricism have epistemological groundings and credentials but that their value in practice was in the manifold ways they could be combined in serious study.

Jevons accomplished all this during a life that lasted only 47 years. He began as a chemist and mathematician, taking a position at age 19 as an assayer in Australia, where he studied first botany and meteorology and then social and economic questions. Returning to England in 1859 after five years, he was given a junior position as a tutor in chemistry in Owens College, Manchester. He soon published a seminal work on mathematical economic theory and another on symbolic logic. He worked later on a logic machine, a precursor to the computer. In 1866 he was made Cobden Professor of Logic, Mental and Moral Philosophy at Owens College. In 1872 he was elected a Fellow of the Royal Society and in 1876 he moved to University College, London as Professor of Political Economy. He died in 1882 from drowning while swimming on a vacation.

The State in Relation to Labour was published by Macmillan in a series identified as dealing with "The English Citizen: His Rights and Responsibilities." The operative question treated by Jevons was, what were and what should be the rights and responsibilities of the variegated English citizenry—and this becomes a question of the economic role of government in resolving conflicts between different groups of English citizens. This is the thorniest issue in the history of economic thought; much economic theory has been developed to either throw objective light on the matter or to enshrine particular normative positions. For his part, Jevons shrinks from neither candid analysis of English social, political, and economic history and institutions nor an openly pragmatic approach to the economic role of government; in both, he eschews the erection of class or other ideological sentiment into principles of policy.

My favorite lines from the book come from its Preface, wherein Jevons establishes the straightforward tone of the book. He writes that

> I think the time is come when all bitter terms, all class rancour, and all needless reference to former unfortunate occurrences, should be laid aside. The economic errors of trades unions after all are not worse than those which pervaded the commercial, if not the governing classes a generation or two ago. One result which clearly emerges from a calm review is that all classes of society are trades unionists at heart, and differ chiefly in the boldness, ability, and secrecy with which they push their respective interests.

Jevons herein makes explicit that *class* is a central feature of his topic. Implicit therein are at least two further points: first, that the economy of the market is a function of the institutions which form and operate through it, such that markets can be and indeed have been formed to favor one class or interest or another; and second, that conventional arguments typically give effect to the class interests that they serve, whether or not they are recognized to be doing so.

Earlier in the Preface, Jevons raises the conundrum that "we uphold the rule of *laissez faire*, and yet in large classes of cases invoke the interference of local or central authorities." He remarks that this "question involves the most delicate and complicated considerations," and argues, "we can lay down no hard-and-fast rules, but must treat every case in detail upon its merits." We can rely on experience, sometimes even on experiment, but "the real difficulty often consists in the interpretation of experience." Experience, in short, does not identify itself; experience is given meaning on the basis of selective perception, that most notably of class position.

Implicit in Jevons's analysis, it seems to me, is an understanding that *some* law, *some* set of legal rights and limitations, must be in place, that the issue is not whether government will establish relative rights and responsibilities but what they will be and, further, when they will be changed. Jevons's analyses, I must point out in a personal aside, many years ago helped me better appreciate that "intervention" normally does not signify the intrusion of government into an area in which it hitherto has been absent but a change in the interests to which government is used to support. This is in addition, of course, to the insight that *some* law must exist in order to have markets, exchange, production, and so on. Without this appreciation, one is relatively susceptible to the introduction of selective normative premises presuming one set of interests or another.

In the first chapter, Jevons rejects the unequivocal use of general abstract, even metaphysical principles and concepts, as difficult as such may be. "Liberty" is a popular theme and laws purporting to help labour can be interpreted as limiting workers' choices. But liberty is a function of the total structure of rights and the laws governing rights, though often spoken of in terms of abstract principles of justice, are, he says, "but a series of arbitrary rules, accumulated or varied from century to century, and defining the terms on which people may best live in each other's company. It is a system of adjustments and compromises, founded upon experience and trial."

Accordingly, he rejects the absolutist theory of property. The first step, he argues, "is to throw aside all supposed absolute rights or inflexible principles. The fact is that legislation is not a science at all; ... It is a matter of practical work, creating human institutions." If we are to understand what law and government is all about, we must, he stresses, "descend from vague terms and abstractions to the definite facts which they imply or are founded upon. We cannot help speaking of principles and rights," he continues, "but we must endeavour to avoid the persistent fallacy of taking words for things." On the one hand, Jevons warns against reification and the naturalist fallacy; on the other, he affirms that the words in which principles and rights—such as "liberty" and "property"—are expressed have been given varying meaning and application—in this he anticipates one of John R. Commons's arguments in his *Legal Foundations of Capitalism* (also reissued by Transaction).

The fact is, Jevons insists, that "[t]he freedom of one continually resolves itself into the restriction of another, whether by government or by private action. Accordingly, the principle of equal freedom for all provides no sure guiding light. The legislator must therefore choose between alternative restrictions somehow to maximize two intangibles, liberty of action and the greatest happiness." But this Benthamite utilitarian calculation can be used to promote freedom and happiness on the intensive margin—that of those most benefited—or on the extensive margin—the number of people benefited. All this comes to a head in his statement that "So intricate are the ways, industrial, sanitary, or political, in which one class or section of the people affect other classes or sections, that there is hardly any limit to the interference of the legislator."

Jevons is especially condemnatory of the invocation of supposed metaphysical absolutes:

> It is futile to uphold, in regard to social legislation, any theory of eternal fixed principles or absolute rights. The whole matter becomes a complex calculus of good and evil. All is a question of probability and degree... Lawgivers, as well as philosophers, delight in discovering euphemisms adapted to maintain the fiction of universal principles...
>
> I venture to maintain, however, that we shall do much better in the end if we throw off the incubus of metaphysical ideas and expressions...
>
> ...Every single act ought to be judged separately as regards the balance of good or evil which it produces...

The good versus evil comparison is a matter of judgment, and requires consideration, given conflicting interests, of whose interest government is to promote:

> Every private Act of Parliament is a distinct interference with some persons for the good of oth-

> ers... There arises an inevitable contest between the private and so to say the public conscience.

The legislator must take a combined empirical, normative, and pragmatic approach; at bottom are further combinations: those combining judgments as to whose interest is to count with judgments as to probabilities [what later came to be called Marshallian statements of tendencies] with regard to means and ends.

> The relation of science to social legislation will now become apparent. Each science is an aggregate of natural laws, more or less general; and these laws, when divested of metaphysical wrappings, resolve themselves into probabilities that certain consequences will follow from certain conjunctions of antecedents. Obviously, at whatever end the legislator aims, he must consult all those sciences whose probabilities bear upon this end.

Jevons also considers that governance encompasses more than official government—with the result that one function of the latter is to mediate and chose between different and competing sets of customs (another theme found in Commons's work). "The state," he writes, is

> the least of the powers that govern us. Whether in the home, the school, the workshop, or the public meeting, we are really governed by an indefinite amount of common law. More especially is this the case in the factory and the exchange. Men of the same trade cannot meet together without entering into some kind of combination, tending to govern its constituents and to affect the interests of outsiders. Industrial society is, and always has been,

> more or less honeycombed with cliques and corners and cabals, each with its own ideas of private interest, and its own code of right and wrong.

When it comes to labour legislation, therefore,

> The relation of the State to labour is a question not so much of the direct restraint of the labourer by the State, as of the manner in which the State can regard the voluntary and unauthorised legislation of the labourers themselves. It may be that the work of the State will consist in increasing rather than lessening the liberty of the individual workman. In any case, it is impossible to treat of industrial legislation without fully taking into account the rules and restraints under which labour exists.

The forgoing are the arguments of the first chapter. These arguments form the framework on which rest the analyses of the ensuing chapters. These chapters deal with direct and indirect interference by the state with employees and employers, and the laws governing trade unions, industrial conspiracy, co-operation and industrial partnership, and arbitration and conciliation.

One consequence of Jevons's approach, coupled with his candor, is his admonition that

> the great lesson which we learn, and it an impressive one, is that legislation with regard to labour has almost always been class legislation. It is the effort of some dominant body to keep down a lower class, which had begun to show inconvenient aspirations.

One of the functions of the use by interested parties of supposedly general transcendent principles is to obfuscate while giving effect to the class-interest basis of actual legislation.

One example Jevons gives is sumptuary laws that "were mere class laws, intended to support the pride of an aristocracy by restraining the tastes of the lower classes." But these laws are to be distinguished from both modern sanitary and consumer protection legislation as well as protective labour legislation, which have as their object "the health and welfare of the people at large" and not the interest of a single class or trade.

(Lest the reader feel that the class nature of sumptuary legislation is a matter solely or even primarily of interpretation, attention is drawn to the *Records of the Governor and Company of the Massachusetts Bay in New England*, Vol. IV, Part I, 1650-1660, pp. 60-61 [Boston: Press of William White, Printer to the Commonwealth, 1854; the spelling has been modernized by me]. The governing body, part legislature and part court, is recorded as holding the following—remarkable, perhaps, less for its specific content and more for its bluntness and candor in the manner in which a Puritanism ostensibly applicable to all persons is brought severely to bear on those of "mean condition" as well as for the elaborate manner of policing provided:

> Although several declarations and orders have been made by this Court against excess in apparel, both of men and women, which have not taken that effect as were to be desired, but, on the contrary, we cannot but to our grief take notice that intolerable excess and bravery hath crept in upon us, and especially amongst people of mean condition, to the dishonor of

God, the scandal of our profession, the consumption of estates, and altogether unsuitable to our poverty; and although we acknowledge it to be a matter of much difficulty, ... yet we cannot but account it our duty to commend unto all sorts of persons the sober and moderate use of those blessings which, beyond expectation, the Lord hath been pleased to afford unto us in this wilderness, and also to declare our utter detestation and dislike that men or women of mean condition should take upon them the garb of gentlemen, by wearing gold or silver lace or buttons, or points at their knees, or to walk in great boots, or women of the same rank to wear silk or tiffany hoods or scarves, which though allowable to persons of greater estates, or more liberal education, yet we cannot but judge it intolerable in persons of such like condition; it is therefore ordered by this Court, and the authority thereof, no person within this jurisdiction, or any of their relations depending upon them, whose visible estates, real and personal, shall not exceed the true and indifferent value of two hundred pounds, shall wear any gold or silver lace, or gold and silver buttons, or any bone lace above two shillings per yard, or silk hoods or scarves, upon the penalty of ten shillings for every such offence, and every such delinquent is to be presented by the grand jury. And forasmuch as distinct and particular rules in this case, suitable to the estate or quality of each person, cannot easily be given, it is further ordered ... that the selectmen of every town, or the major part of them, are hereby enabled and required from time to time to have regard and taken notice of apparel in any of the inhabitants of their several towns respectively, and whosoever they shall judge to exceed their

> ranks and abilities in the costliness or fashion of their apparel in any respect, ... the selectmen aforesaid shall have power to assess such persons so offending ... in the country rates at two hundred pounds estates, according to that proportion that such men use to pay to whom such apparel is suitable and allowed, provided this law shall not extend to the restraint of any magistrate or public officer of the jurisdiction, their wives and children, who are left to their discretion in wearing of apparel, or any settled military officer or soldier in the time of military service, or any other whose education and employments have been above the ordinary degree, or whose estates have been considerable, though now decayed.

In 1958 I attended a bankers conference in Columbia, Missouri, in which one group firmly believed that bank accounts and other client relations should be available only to propertied/wealthy people.)

These and other laws relating to labour cannot be "decided once for all on some supposed principle of liberty." The questions to which they related must be treated "on the varied and detailed grounds of expedience." Arguments about "abstract indefeasible right" cannot be settled; but legislation is a matter of circumstance, and must be guided by experience, and pragmatic and expedient (means-ends) judgments can be made.

One conspicuous problem, of course, is that much if not all legislation can be described in terms favorable to both some group and some general interest. From Jevons's point of view, here is where judgments of subtle discrimination must be made.

Economists, in Jevons's view, have both misunderstood and perverted the relevance of the theories of production and distribution. These theories do not unequivocally militate in favor of one set of labour arrangements rather than another—however much interested parties and some biased economists have held to the contrary. Although many questions devolve into complex cases of the laws of supply and demand, there is nothing unequivocal about those laws, or about the laws of distribution, such as the wages fund theory, which establishes the whole amount to be divided, the proportionate share which any particular labourer may obtain, the relation of the theory to actual institutions, or the question of the proper institutions of the labour market.

Jevons considers the supposition of a conflict between labour and capital to be a delusion. "The real conflict is between producers and consumers." Both capitalist and labour restrictions on output constitute the levying of private taxation on consumers. And not all workers are equally situated to form unions. "As in so many other walks of life, to him that hath shall be given."

Jevons considers the chequered history of repression of trade unions, the good and evil of strikes, and similar issues, typically noting the difficulties that ensue from varying interpretations of experience. Still, he does not hesitate to refer to the legal and medical professions as "governed by elaborate systems of social terrorism"—rather strong language for his time and place—though he distinguishes them from other unions.

Among other things, Jevons raises the question of "industrial treason." He says, on the one hand, "a great strike, if carried sufficiently far, might assume the character of social treason," and on the other, that "it is one thing to hold that there must exist the offence of conspiracy, and another thing to say that any particular kind of conspiracy should be punished." Distinctions must be made on pragmatic grounds; "the essence of illegality is injury to other people," but the determination of injury and of evidence of injury is a matter of selective perception, and Jevons understandably does not try to provide a set of criteria for drawing distinctions.

Indeed, conspiracy is not the only mode of approaching the subject; Jevons suggests that "[i]t is quite in accordance with all precedents that every citizen should be bound to perform duties essential to the good of the State and the community." Of course, this approach, too, is not conclusive: The appeal to "all precedents" is dubious; distinctions can be made between the domain of obligation and that of voluntary benevolence; and, most especially, both what is "essential" to the good and what is "good" are matters of selective perception.

Even in modern liberal social democracies, some notion of "essential" services—whether in the context of a union strike ("national emergency" strikes") or a "shutdown" of government services (for example, as a political ploy)—is common. Jevons argues that "there should be some legal authority capable in the last resort of obliging citizens to perform certain essential duties, whether it be the stoking of gas retorts, the mending of water conduits, or the mining of coal, essential for the life of the nation." He notes (in the 3rd edition of 1894, pp. 140-141) that "the great railway strike in the United States, which was, in fact, an industrial insurrection, was brought to an end not by any legal process, but by the arbitrary exhibition of force." (Some years later he could have cited the election to the presidency of a man who ended a police strike.) But Jevons would not have such a policy with regard to services deemed essential extend more broadly, say, to prohibit all exercise of union withholding power. He quotes a report of members of a Royal Commission in 1867: "It seems to us that the policy of imposing exceptional penalties upon the labouring population *en masse*, and as such recognizing in that class exceptional offences, is a principle vicious in itself, and long discredited. Nothing but some extraordinary danger to the public safety, or some peculiar proneness to crime, can justify an anomalous system. We can see nothing in the combination of workmen which the ordinary policy cannot deal with." In other words, reasoned and measured exercise of social control is preferred to repressive class legislation.

Jevons holds that labour-capital relations is a matter of adopting suitable institutions—institutions evidently in the sense not only of appropriate organizations and laws but of reasonable settled habits of belief and expectation. "There can be no doubt," he writes, "that the soundest possible solution of the labour question will eventually be found in such a modification of the terms of partnership as shall bind the interests of the employer and workman more closely together." He might have resonated warmly with the view of organizers of the hitherto disadvantaged that "reconciliation" will arise when the disadvantaged get some meaningful power and the hitherto advantage get reconciled to that fact.

Perhaps most interestingly, Jevons the economic theorist makes an entry. A third of the way into Chapter VII, Jevons notes that the laws of supply and demand—which he associates with pure competition—"do not apply" *inter alia* to cases of collective bargaining. He raises the possibility of a deadlock and, citing F. Y. Edgeworth's *Mathematical Psychics* (1881) (which he mistakenly calls Physics) raises the bedeviling problem of indeterminacy—all in the service of suggesting a useful role for a conciliator "on the grounds of pure economic theory."

What is unequivocally clear is that Jevons is endeavoring to accommodate the reasonable interests of workers while avoiding the repressive extremes of past class legislation, i.e., to not blindly and uncaringly promote the interests of any class.

In his concluding remarks, Jevons acknowledges how "hesitating and conflicting, if not positively contradictory" his results may appear. Such a view, he suggests, is superficial. It arises because he has sought to avoid extremes and to apply discrimination. "Restrictions on industry," he writes, "are not good or bad *per se*, but according as they are imposed wisely and with good intentions, or foolishly, and with sinister intentions." He seeks what some think is impossible, substantively or logically, namely, "a definite improvement in some class of people without injuring others." It is all, or in large part, a matter of the beliefs and expectations that help form the sense of interest by individuals and classes. To that end, admitting "there can be no royal road to legislation in such matters," he calls, in part, for caution and learning from experience:

> We must neither maximize the functions of government at the beck of quasi-military officials,

nor minimize them according to the theories of the very best philosophers. We must learn to judge each case upon its merits, interpreting with painful care all experience which can be brought to bear upon the matter.

Jevons might have called for the application of Adam Smith's insights into the workings of the principles of approbation and disapprobation of our own and of others' conduct. He did not, but he does call for both the pragmatism of case-by-case treatment and tolerance, the latter of which is "indispensable," all in the service of the good of all the people. Neither classical political economy nor neoclassical economics nor Jevons himself provided an unequivocally sharper strategy. But what he says is consistent with and indeed represents the best of the approach taken by the mainstream of cosmopolitan and humanitarian economists since Smith to questions of economic policy and the economic role of government—a far cry from the classist (mis)uses of economic doctrines.

Warren J. Samuels

PREFACE

So much has been written about Labour and Capital and the legislation relating to them that it is scarcely possible to say anything new upon this subject. Not only is there an immense literature of controversial pamphlets bearing upon the matter, but there is also a superabundance of facts and information. What seems now to be needed is a careful attempt to understand the principles of legislation which emerge when we analyse the actions of the Legislature, and the state of public opinion with reference to the conflict of labour and capital and the regulation of industry. The all-important point is to explain if possible why, in general, we uphold the rule of *laisser faire,* and yet in large classes of cases invoke the interference of local or central authorities. This question involves the most delicate and complicated considerations, and the outcome of the inquiry is that we can lay down no hard-and-fast rules, but must treat every case in detail upon its merits. Specific experience is our best guide, or even express experiment where possible; but the real difficulty often consists in the interpretation of experience. We are reduced to balance conflicting probabilities of good and evil. In order, however, to prevent the possible misapprehensions into which a hasty reader of some of the following pages might fall, I may here state that I am a thorough-going advocate of free trade. As the subject of the book does not include foreign commerce I have no opportunity of showing the consistency of this doctrine with such regulation of home industry as I advocate.

Concerning the functions and actions of trade societies I have not hesitated to express approval or blame in the freest way; but I think the time is come when all bitter terms, all class rancour, and all needless reference to former unfortunate occurrences, should be laid aside. The economic errors of trades unions after all are not worse than those which pervaded the commercial, if not the governing classes a generation or two ago. One result which clearly emerges from a calm review is that all classes of society are trades unionists at heart, and differ chiefly in the boldness, ability, and secrecy with which they push their respective interests.

The necessity of writing briefly has generally prevented me from giving references to authors or quotations of facts and opinions. I must content myself with acknowledging my special indebtedness to certain works—such as Professor F. A. Walker's *Wages Question;* Mr. George Howell's *Conflicts of Capital and Labour;* Mr. G. J. Holyoake's instructive and amusing *History of Co-operation;* Mr. J. E. Davis' excellent treatise on the Labour Laws; Mr. Jos. D. Weeks' Reports on the Practical Operation of Arbitration and Conciliation (Harrisburg, U.S.A.); the valuable collection of documents contained in the Report on Trades Societies, published by the Social Science Association in 1860; the eleven voluminous reports of the Trades Union Commissioners of 1867, especially the masterly memorandum of Sir William Erle upon the Law relating to Trades Unions; the Reports of the Labour Laws Commission of 1874, of the Factory Acts Commission, the Factory Inspectors, etc.

HAMPSTEAD, N.W.
April 1882.

THE STATE IN RELATION TO LABOUR

CHAPTER I

PRINCIPLES OF INDUSTRIAL LEGISLATION

WE are about to deal in this little Treatise with the proper methods and limits of legislation in matters relating to labour—that is to say, the operative or handicraft classes. We have to distinguish, as far as possible, between cases in which individuals should be left at liberty, as being the best judges of their own interests, and those cases in which some kind of authority should interfere, in order to insure or increase their welfare. Imagine, for the sake of illustration, that there is in some factory a piece of revolving machinery which is likely to crush to death any person carelessly approaching it. Here is a palpable evil which it would be unquestionably well to avert by some means or other. But by what means? It is obvious that there are many possible courses to choose between, and much to be said for and against each particular course.

In the first place, it may fairly be said that the

individual workman is bound to take care of himself, and to be especially wary when approaching machinery. Mere common sense, we might think, would lead people to avoid negligent conduct likely to be instantly and inexorably punished with sudden death, or the most fearful and painful mutilation. As a general rule, at least, adult persons must take care of themselves, and observe where they are going. If everybody is to go in leading-strings, it is obvious that there will be no persons left to act as leaders. It may well be urged, too, that the more we guard people from palpable dangers, the more heedless they will become, and the more likely to fall victims to some unforeseen danger. But a little observation and reflection show that to such general rules and arguments there must be exceptions. It is all very well for theorists and "cabinet philosophers" to argue about what people ought to do; but if we learn from unquestionable statistical returns that thousands of hapless persons do, as a matter of fact, get crushed to death, or variously maimed, by unfenced machinery, these are calamities which no theory can mitigate.

Evidently there must be cases where it is incumbent on one citizen to guard against danger to other citizens. If one man digs a pit in search of coal, and, not finding coal, leaves the hole uncovered, to be half hidden by grass and brambles, he is laying a mere trap for his neighbours; he might as well at once lay man-traps and spring-guns in the old-fashioned way. Are all neighbours to grope their way about in constant fear of a horrible, lingering death, because he dislikes the trouble of filling up or covering the pit he has made? So obviously unreasonable was such neglect, that we find a customary law existing in the Forest of Dean two hundred years ago, requiring every owner of an abandoned pit to cover it over. Now, revolving machinery is in many cases quite on a par with uncovered coal-pits. When the putting up, at inconsiderable expense, of a few bars of wood or iron will remove all danger and difficulty, surely it is much better simply to put them up, and avoid all metaphysical argument.

Unfortunately the metaphysician cannot be kept at bay in so simple a way. Having once decided that the fly-wheel ought to be fenced, we have but raised a series of questions relating to the person who ought to put up the fences, and the other persons who have either a right or a duty to take care that he puts them up. We might, in the first place, assume that the owner of dangerous machinery would fence it from motives of mere humanity, if not from those of self-interest. But here again experience proves the existence of unaccountable thoughtlessness, if not heartlessness. Before the Legislature began to interfere, hardly any owner of machinery thought of incurring the small additional percentage of cost requisite to render the machinery safe to the operatives. Plenty of documentary evidence exists, moreover, to show that legislation on the subject was distinctly opposed by factory owners. In other cases mere thoughtlessness and indifference can alone be charged against the owners. In one of the reports of factory inspectors we are told that when the inspector remonstrated against the dangerous unfenced condition of a fly-wheel, the owner calmly remarked that it had no doubt killed a man not long before; he made no objection to erecting the necessary fence, the idea of which did not seem to have previously occurred to his mind.

It is obvious, then, that somebody ought to suggest ideas of the sort to the erectors of dangerous machine traps. But there is still a wide choice of means and persons. The men employed about the factory might be expected to meet together and, through their trades union or otherwise, insist upon proper fences being put up. But, as a matter of fact, the men have not generally taken this reasonable course. Whether from false pride, want of thought, or otherwise, the last people to complain about danger seem to be the people exposed to it. The public in general, through the agency of some society such as the Royal Humane Society, might be expected to step in from humanitarian motives, and either fence the machinery at their own cost, or oblige the owners to do it. But there is nothing more fickle and unaccountable than the humanity of the public in general. The Legislature might frighten the owner of machinery into carefulness by making negligence into manslaughter, should a fatal accident occur. Judges and juries might do much to the same end by awarding heavy damages against the owner. But there remains one other mode of solving the question which is as simple as it is effective. The law may command that dangerous machinery shall be fenced, and the executive government may appoint inspectors to go round and prosecute such owners as disobey the law.

The Principle of Liberty.—Of course the case treated above is but a simple example of the questions which arise in every matter relating to the health, safety, convenience, or general welfare of the workman. If an employer offers a man work in a very unhealthy workshop, and the man accepts the work and its conditions, are the employer and the workman at perfect liberty to carry out such a contract? Has the community nothing to say to the matter. Is the Legislature to save the man from sudden death by the rotating fly-wheel, and yet to leave him, unwarned and unaided, to a slower but surer death by steel particles, phosphorus vapour, clay dust, lead poisoning, or some other easily avoidable source of injury? The answer no doubt may depend upon the question whether the operative is an adult man, an adult woman, a young person (*i.e.* a boy or girl of the age of fourteen years and under eighteen years), or a helpless child. But, even in the extreme case of the adult man, experience unquestionably shows that men from mere thoughtlessness or ignorance incur grave injuries to health or limb which very little pressure from the Legislature would avert with benefit to all parties. The difficult question thus arises whether, out of respect to some supposed principle of individual liberty, the State ought to allow men to go on working and living in the midst of needless risks.

It may well be urged, on the one hand, that the liberty of the subject is an indefeasible right of Englishmen, and a fundamental principle of English law. Not only is liberty in itself a prime element in happiness, but it is also the necessary condition of that free development from which all our social blessings arise. Liberty is a theme upon which it would be possible to enlarge very considerably, and it is always a popular theme.

But if my study of this subject has led to any true

results, the first step must be to rid our minds of the idea that there are any such things in social matters as abstract rights, absolute principles, indefeasible laws, inalterable rules, or anything whatever of an eternal and inflexible nature. We deal here, it should be observed, only with a lower class of relations, and have nothing directly to do with those higher questions of ethical science, of moral obligation, of conscience, of religious conviction, in which we may rightly seek for a firmer basis. Legislation undoubtedly must take account of moral feelings, and must usually conform to the prevailing opinions of the people. Yet a positive law is a very different thing from a moral rule: the former deals only with outward acts; the latter both with acts and motives. Not uncommonly conflict arises. A nonconformist refuses to pay church-rates or Easter offerings; a clergyman declines to recognise the authority of a temporal court; an anti-vaccinationist prefers fine and imprisonment to allowing a slight but life-saving operation on his children; one of the "peculiar people" goes still further, and maintains that it is the law of God not to call in a physician to a dying child. All these cases raise very difficult questions; but the attitude of the law is simple. Either the man does as the law orders, or he goes to prison. A person may entertain whatever moral feelings he thinks proper to indulge in, and in our present state of society he enjoys the further liberty of expressing those feelings nearly *but not quite* without limits. Hence he enjoys the privilege, in England at least, of endeavouring to persuade other people that the law is mistaken. If he succeeds, it is well; if not, he must practically conform.

But the law in itself has nothing to do with conscience, nor religion, nor even with moral right and wrong, as estimated by individuals. Moreover, it knows nothing of absolute principles from which we must not diverge. It is but a series of arbitrary rules, accumulated or varied from century to century, and defining the terms on which people may best live in each other's society. It is a system of adjustments and compromises, founded upon experience and trial. The complication of social relations is such that no simple unqualified laws can hold good in all cases; necessary exceptions spring up as soon as ever we try to establish a general proposition. It might surely be thought, for instance, that a man would be free to buy and sell as he thought best. Barter, moreover, being the original simple form of commerce, would *à fortiori* seem to be open to every free subject. Yet, since the fourth year of Edward IV. (cap. 1) laws have existed prohibiting the payment of wages in the manner of barter. Even at the present day the Truck Act is in full operation (1st and 2d William IV. cap. 37), and in a number of specified trades inflicts penalties on any settlement of wages by way of barter, the third offence being treated as a misdemeanour punishable by fine only at the discretion of the court. Curiously enough, however, this law does not apply to agricultural labourers, domestic servants, and various other important classes of the employed. What is a misdemeanour in an iron-work or cotton-mill is the most familiar arrangement possible in the adjoining farmhouse. All that can be said in favour of the law, and it is probably sufficient, is that repeated inquiry and long experience ever since the time of King Edward IV. have shown that masters abuse the liberty of making barter contracts with their workmen. But what becomes of that celebrated entity, "the liberty of the subject"?

It may be imagined, again, that a person has an absolute right to his own property. Apart from the difficulty of defining what is his own property, a cursory examination of the statute-book would show that this absolute right has been invaded in every conceivable way. Taxation is in complete conflict with the supposed absoluteness of the right. Even property in a man's own labour has never been absolute: sailors were pressed into the navy; military service was in former centuries compulsory, as it now is in most continental countries, and in theory yet is in England; statute labour was required to mend the roads. The compulsory purchase of land for railways, water-works, and other enterprises of public utility, is a further invasion of absolute rights, although accompanied in most cases by abundant, if not superfluous compensation. The new Irish Land Act is destructive to the absolutist theory, as regards Ireland at least; that Act has been denounced as contrary to all the principles of political economy. But when a country has arrived at a state of social disorganisation, the probabilities of good implied in those principles are met by certainty of evil, and the question simply is by what least sacrifice to approximate to a sounder state of things.

There is, indeed, no subject more generally misconceived than the relation which exists between economics and legislation. It is generally supposed that the economist is a presumptuous theorist, who is continually laying down hard-and-fast rules for the conduct of other people.

Everybody is to buy in the cheapest market, and sell in the dearest; marriage is to be restrained as much as possible; paupers are to be reduced to the verge of starvation; strikes are not to be endured, and so forth. It is possible that such ideas may have been put forward by some over-dogmatic economist such as MacCulloch. For the most part, however, they arise from the misinterpretation by the public of the relation between science and practice. It is one thing to demonstrate scientifically the tendency of population to progress in a geometric ratio; it is quite another thing to infer that marriage should therefore be discouraged, still more that it should be discouraged by some particular measure, which might involve consequences of the most varied character.

As, then, in philosophy the first step is to begin by doubting everything, so in social philosophy, or rather in practical legislation, the first step is to throw aside all supposed absolute rights or inflexible principles. The fact is that legislation is not a science at all; it is no more a science than the making of a ship or a steam-engine, or an electrical machine, is a science. It is a matter of practical work, creating human institutions. There are sciences which instruct us in the making of a ship or an engine, and which, by giving us comprehension of its nature, enable us to use it well or to improve it. In these sciences there may be general principles of nature. So there may be general sciences of ethics, of economics, of jurisprudence, which may much assist us in the work of legislation. But before we can bring the principles down to practice they run into infinite complications, and break up into all kinds of exceptions and apparent anomalies.

Abstractions and Realities.—In endeavouring to gain clear ideas as to the proper method of legislation, nothing is more necessary than to descend from vague terms and abstractions to the definite facts which they imply or are founded upon. We cannot help speaking of principles and rights, but we must endeavour to avoid the persistent fallacy of taking words for things. Such principles are not existing things; they are only complex propositions founded on extensive experience, and indicating the probable results of actions. They are registers, as it were, of the convictions of society that a certain course will involve certain consequences. The principle of the common law, for instance, that parents have a right to the governance of their children, is a register of the general belief that the strong instinctive love of parent for child will be the best guarantee in general for the beneficial treatment of the child, while conducing also to the happiness of the parents. Mathematically speaking, there is a large balance of probability of good in favour of the law. But it can never have been intended that a right designed for the production of good should be perverted to the production of evil. Probability cannot stand against certainty. If it clearly appear that a parent is injuring his child, there is an end of presumption to the contrary, and it is a mere question of degree when the power of the law will step in to prevent this injury. To preserve an appearance of consistency the lawyers use various circumlocutions.

A parent has the legal right of chastising his child; but this does not mean that he may beat his child whenever he feels inclined; as the lawyers say, the chastisement must be reasonable; which, being interpreted, means that the parent must never chastise his child but in such manner, degree, and on such occasion (if any there be) as is conducive to the good of the child primarily, with some regard, perhaps, to the interests of the family and neighbours secondarily. In fact, it comes to this, that he has no right to do anything but just what he ought to do, all the circumstances being taken into account. So from time to time, as it was made plain that children were being worked to death in factories—reduced to crippled, stunted, deformed little creatures—a further inroad was made upon the parent's right. The presumption of good was altogether rebutted by the certainty of evil, and the State undertook, through the Factory Acts, to secure a better state of things. Quite recently the same conflict between presumed good and certain evil arose in the controversy regarding elementary education. The parent in theory was the best educational guardian of the child; but, if the result was no education at all, there was no ground for the theory. In this case, again, the State dispersed metaphysics by stepping in and ordering the child to be educated.

Grounds and Limits of Legislation.—It may be fearlessly said that no social transformation would be too great to be commended and attempted if only it could be clearly shown to lead to the greater happiness of the community. No scheme of Bellers, or Babeuf, or Robert Owen could be resisted, if only their advocates could adduce scientific evidence of their practicability and good tendency. No laws, no customs, no rights of property are so sacred that they may not be made away with, if it can be clearly shown that they stand in the way of the greatest happiness. *Salus populi, suprema lex.* But it ought to be evident that before we venture upon a great leap in the dark, we may well ask for cogent evidence as to the character of the landing-place. The question resolves itself into one of logic. What are the means of proving inductively or deductively that a certain change will conduce to the greater sum of happiness? In the case of any novel and considerable change direct experience must be wanting. The present social arrangements have the considerable presumption in their favour that they can at least exist, and they can be tolerated. A heavy burden of proof, therefore, lies upon him who would advocate any social change which has not or cannot be tested previously on a small scale. Wherever direct experience can assure us that good is to be obtained by a certain course, we may with some confidence venture to adopt it. In hardly any case, however, are the consequences of an action or a law limited to the direct obvious results. As Bastiat said, we must take into account "what is not seen" as well as "what is seen."

To descend, however, from philosophy to the practical subject before us, I conceive that the State is justified in passing any law, or even in doing any single act which, without ulterior consequences, adds to the sum total of happiness. Good done is sufficient justification of any act, in the absence of evidence that equal or greater evil will subsequently follow. It is no doubt a gross interference with that metaphysical entity, the liberty of the subject, to prevent a man from working with phosphorus as he pleases. But if it can be shown by unquestionable statistics and the unimpeachable evidence of scientific men that such working with phosphorus leads to a dreadful disease, easily preventable by a small change of procedure, then I hold that the Legislature is *primâ facie* justified in obliging the man to make this small change. The liberty of the subject is only the means towards an end; it is not itself the end; hence, when it fails to produce the desired end, it may be set aside, and other means employed. Wherever, in like manner, palpable evil arises, the Legislature is justified, if not bound to inquire, whether by some special change of law that evil might not be avoided. It is obvious, however, that in this inquiry all effects of the proposed act, whatever be their remoteness or uncertainty, must be taken into account. Direct observation, therefore, will not usually be all-sufficient. There may be collateral or secondary effects of an action which will not be apparent for years to come.

The Evolutionist Doctrine of Freedom.—If we are to acknowledge the existence in social affairs of any indefeasible right or absolute principle, none would seem more sacred than the principle of freedom—the right of the individual to pursue his own course towards his own ideal end. In favour of such a view, it may be said, in the first place, that happiness mainly consists in unimpeded and successful energising. Every needless check or limitation of action amounts to so much destruction of pleasurable energy, or chance of such. Not only, however, must man, in common with the brutes, suffer from endless material checks and obstacles, but he cannot enjoy the society of other men without constantly coming into conflict with them. The freedom of one continually resolves itself into the restriction of another. In any case, then, the mere fact of society existing obliges us to admit the necessity of laws, not designed, indeed, to limit the freedom of any one person, except so far as this limitation tends on the whole to the greater average freedom of all. Thus the evolutionists aim, not so much at directly maximising happiness, as at maximising liberty of action, which they conceive to be equivalent to the means of greatest happiness. The principle of equal freedom is therefore put forth as an all-extensive and sure guide in social matters. It would lead me too far to attempt in this place to inquire whether the present course of industrial legislation, and the remarks to be made upon it in the present volume, are really reconcilable with this principle. I am inclined to think that the reconciliation is not impossible; but that, when applied to the vast communities of modern society, the principle fails to give a sure guiding light. So intricate are the ways, industrial, sanitary, or political, in which one class or section of the people affect other classes or sections, that there is hardly any limit to the interference of the legislator.

I do not think that such interference, applying, as it would do, only to the simpler physical conditions of the body, can be said, in a reasonable point of view, to diminish freedom. As physical conditions become more regulated, the intellectual and emotional nature of man expands ever more freely. The modern English citizen who lives under the burden of the revised edition of the Statutes, not to speak of innumerable municipal, railroad, sanitary, and other bye-laws, is after all an infinitely freer as well as nobler creature than the savage who is always under the despotism of physical want. He is far freer, too, than the poor Indian who, though perhaps unacquainted with written law, is bound down by the most inflexible system of traditional usage and superstition. It is impossible, in short, that we can have the constant multiplication of institutions and instruments of civilisation which evolution is producing, without a growing complication of relations, and a consequent growth of social regulations.

The doctrines of evolution, moreover, are yet so young and novel, being, indeed, no older than illustrious philosophers yet living and working among us, that it is hardly to be supposed that the full bearing of such doctrines should yet be appreciated, even by their originators. It is easy to perceive that in many a primitive community little legislative interference is needed, because the people, by long-continued trial, have settled down to a mode of life approximately perfect according to its circumstances. There long tradition is legislation, and often legislation of the most strict and minute kind. Evolution has had time to work its full effects; we see it accomplished, not in progress. But all is different with a great modern manufacturing community, the whole mode of industry and life of which has been invented or profoundly modified within the memory of men yet living or but lately dead. Tradition is in such a case broken and dispersed. New conditions of life have to be discovered and tried. Evolution is doubtless at work, but the question arises whether the very legislation which we are about to consider is not the manifestation of evolution. Based, at any rate, upon trial and experience, it is but the multiplying of the good tendencies, and the quick elimination of the bad. It is an attempt to save needless suffering by making the few teach the many, so as to bring individuals into conformity with their environment without the blind striving of individual action.

The Metaphysical Incubus.—It is futile to attempt to uphold, in regard to social legislation, any theory of eternal fixed principles or abstract rights. The whole matter becomes a complex calculus of good and evil. All is a question of probability and degree. A rule of law is grounded on a recognised probability of good arising in the opinion of the lawgiver from a certain line of conduct. But as there almost always occur cases in which this tendency to good is overmastered by some opposite tendency, the lawgiver proceeds to enact new rules limiting, as it is said, but in reality reversing, the former one in special cases. Lawgivers, as well as philosophers, delight in discovering euphemisms adapted to maintain the fiction of universal principles. When the principles fail to hold good, it is said that the cases are exceptional. It is a general principle that a man may do as he likes with his own property. It is an exception when a railway company forcibly takes possession of his land.

I venture to maintain, however, that we shall do much better in the end if we throw off the incubus of metaphysical ideas and expressions. We must resolve all these supposed principles and rights into the facts and probabilities which they are found to involve when we inquire into their real meaning. The right of a man to dispose freely of his labour means the recognition by the Legislature that in the majority of cases a man is the best judge of his own interests in disposing of his labour. In a number of cases specified in the statute-books, the Legislature recognises an opposite state of things. The principle of the freedom of trade stands on the same footing; it is a probability of advantage which, however, must be set aside in case of greater probability of evil. The indefeasible right of a squire to his ancestral acres rests, of course, upon the like considerations. All depend ultimately upon the *salus populi*, which is the only *lex suprema.*

The question may well arise, indeed, whether, according to the doctrine here upheld, there is really any place at all for rules and general propositions. If a general law may be limited by a particular law, and that again by a further and more limited exception, we shall get down eventually to individual cases. When followed out, this is the outcome of the Benthamist doctrine. Every single act ought to be judged separately as regards the balance of good or evil which it produces. Practically, too, the doctrine is often recognised as true and necessary. Many Acts of Parliament give discretionary power to the Secretary of State, so that he can deal with each individual case acording to its merits. Under the Factory and Workshop Act of 1878, extensive powers of relaxing the directions of the Act are given to the Secretary of State. Many of the sections contain a clause beginning, "Where it is proved to the satisfaction of a Secretary of State," etc. Thus section 43 gives power to allow the period of employment to be between 9 A.M. and 9 P.M. in certain cases.

It will be easily seen, however, that legislation becomes impracticable when it runs into too much detail. Not only is discretionary action likely to be abused, but the time and trouble spent in obtaining it form a considerable obstacle. There arises a distinct advantage in being able to know how other people will act, and whether they are or are not acting rightly. Even under a system of general rules, such as are most of those contained in the statute-book, legislation is so complex that only those who give themselves wholly to the study can be acquainted with any considerable part of it. The statute-book, again, can never really contain the whole of the law, as the definitions of terms, the conflicts of clauses and acts, the complex evolution of unforeseen cases, necessitate numberless decisions which practically add themselves to the text.

Inferential Results of Legislation.—Among the most important effects of a legislative act must be placed the expectations which it creates of future similar or apparently similar acts. People are always reasoning, well or ill—usually ill. Accordingly, every conspicuous act which is done becomes a precedent, on which many future claims are based. In courts of law where that metaphysical entity justice is administered, judges are obliged to act upon precedents. The expectations raised and the actions guided by one decision must be justified by a like decision in similar circumstances. This is done even when the particular decision is regretted by the judges and allowed to work evil in itself. It is impossible, however, that law can be administered otherwise than by reference to precedents, and the only question remaining open is the minuteness of analysis of the circumstances and conditions. As no two exactly similar cases ever do come before courts of law, analysis, if carried to the utmost, would practically render every decision independent of every other decision;—there never can, in short, be a precise precedent. Practically, therefore, the analysis of precedents is restricted to those more obvious elements which can be generally apprehended, and, in jury cases, rendered satisfactory to the average British householder.

The Legislature is less bound by regard to precedent. It is all powerful, and apparently irresponsible. It can do single executive acts as well as pass general rules of law. Every private Act of Parliament is a distinct interference with some persons for the good of others. In special cases it acts for the good of a single individual—reversing a legal decision, validifying a questionable marriage, rectifying accidental mistakes, authorising the enclosure of land, or altering the legal status of a single estate. These well-understood cases bear out my contention that any act is justified by the good done in the absence of countervailing inferential or other evils. But even in regard to private acts, Parliament is to a great extent bound by tradition and precedent. Such acts generally fall into well-defined classes with regard to which experience has already been gained. Any proposal for a novel kind of private act meets with the utmost scrutiny. Railway companies, for instance, seem able to obtain almost any land they want for their purposes. They have merely to ask, and it is given at a price. But when a company proposed to build a large hotel near Lincoln's Inn, and applied for a private act to enable them to make the purchase of land, the Bill was summarily rejected by the Lords. In this particular case the public would probably have gained distinct benefit from the passing of the Act. The result of course would have been that multitudes of other companies would discover modes of benefiting the public by building hotels and other large structures by private Acts of Parliament. In this way it is that we become hampered in every act of legislation, if not of private life. We must do to one as we would to another, or else we must be prepared to give some clear reason why we do not. This reason, too, must be clear and sufficient, not so much to those who act, as to those who are in a position to judge the actors. The distinctions, then, must not be very fine drawn. Public opinion is in the highest degree undiscriminating, and yet it is the ultimate court of appeal. Thus the legislator or the administrator may be practically compelled to abstain from many measures and acts good in themselves, because if they happened to come under public notice they would not be discriminated from measures and acts of a recognised evil tendency. It necessarily follows that the public man, without the least real sacrifice of his own conscience and instincts of right, is obliged to defer more or less to the state of public opinion and of popular education There arises an inevitable contest between the private and so to say the public conscience.

Questions of Degree.—One of the most serious difficulties standing in the way of legislation is the fact that many legislative questions are questions of degree. One act differs from another not by any clearly assignable mark present in one and absent in the other, but by more or less of the same mark. In a case of assault, for instance, the provocation given may vary from nothing at all up to something extremely great, and there may be all intermediate degrees. Sir W. Erle, in his profound memorandum upon the Law of Trades Unions, pointed out that in the case of nuisances, whether by obstruction or otherwise, unlawfulness begins at a certain degree of annoyance, and that this degree is to be measured not by any exact standard, but on a supposed estimate of what is reasonable by men assumed to be prudent.

Two obvious difficulties arise out of this variation of degree: the first consists in the fact that it is often impossible to define with certainty what acts are to be restrained by law and what left free. Obstruction of the Queen's highway may range from the case of one or two men carelessly lounging about, up to that of thousands of men purposely blocking the road in order to create public terror and disaster. Negligence, again, is a legal fault of which no precise measure can be given. To shoot a person by misadventure is not criminal in the eye of the law; to shoot him owing to a certain undefined degree of negligence is manslaughter.

A second resulting difficulty consists in the fact that in questions of degree an illegal act must differ by an infinitesimal quantity from a legal act. Mere carelessness merges on one side into pure accident, but on the other side into gross or illegal negligence. Now when an act ceases to be legally innocent, it becomes legally culpable, and in theory there must be some point at which this change logically takes place. At this point the minutest difference distinguishes crime from innocence. It is a case of the ancient logical sophism called the *Sorites* or the *Acervalis.* It can be shown that one single hair makes the difference between a bald man and those well-haired people who have no special class-name, but are not bald. If a man who has only a hundred hairs is called bald, the question will arise whether men with 101, 102, 103, 104 hairs, and so on, are also bald. If so, we can proceed with like questions until we get up to thousands of hairs. Sooner or later the man must be pronounced *not-bald;* but as there is no third term or middle between bald and not-bald, the change must take place upon a single hair. Certainly this is often the case with legal questions. A railway signalman charged with manslaughter on account of some mistake is either committed for trial or not committed: there is no legal middle term. But the mistake occasioning the accident may vary in culpability from zero up to something amounting to murder. At some point, therefore, an infinitesimal difference lies between crime and innocence.

In practice, these nice questions of degree are slurred over, and roughly decided by referring the whole matter to the discretion of a jury. Twelve jurymen decide whether the signalman has used ordinary and reasonable caution, "such as might be fairly expected from a person in his position." The lawyers and the judges are always talking about "what is reasonable," "what is fair," although they know perfectly well that they cannot explain clearly what they mean. Nor can the jury say any better on what clear grounds they decide the question of "reasonable care." Probably, the only real use in the jury system is that it furnishes the judges with a practical measure of ordinary ways of thinking. Unconsciously the twelve men in the jury-box are so many standard measures of ordinary capacity, and though they may differ more or less in opinion, the final average opinion is the best standard of "reasonableness" which we can command. It is curious to observe how frequently men are engaged in solving mathematical problems without being aware of the fact.

Baconian Legislation.—Hardly any person will be found to contest the statement that legislation must proceed upon the ground of experience. Legislation must be Baconian. But, when we try to ascertain exactly what is meant by these statements, difference of opinion will arise. As I have attempted in another book to show, all reasoning must be general. Even when we appear to pass in inference from one single experiment to a like one, we rise in the course of the logical journey to a general truth concerning all such experiments, so far as they are like to each other, and then we descend the logical mountain again to the particular one in prospect. But there may be all degrees of proximateness or remoteness between our real premisses of fact and our ultimate conclusion. What I venture to maintain is that Baconian legislation will always proceed by reasoning from the most nearly proximate and analogous experience which is available. We cannot possibly dispense with general reasoning, but we should use it as sparingly as possible. We should choose, as it were, the lowest logical elevation within sight.

I have recently endeavoured to show, in an article in the *Contemporary Review* of January 1880 (vol. xxxvii. pp.

177-192), that in many cases it is possible for the legislator to resort to direct experiment. Before passing any great Act of Parliament which will involve the whole of an extensive trade or class in some irrevocable and costly change, we ought to try experiments, and thus obtain the most direct and pertinent evidence concerning the probable result. It is not for a moment to be supposed that legislation has not long, or, even always, been based upon experiment or upon experience in some sense; but the experiments have generally been the unintentional changes which time and circumstance have wrought, or the institutions which individuals or private societies have created with no distinct legislative purpose. The vast collection of parliamentary papers which Parliament has printed in the last hundred years, amounting to several thousand folio volumes, show the empirical basis upon which the Legislature has proceeded. Not a few great laws, notably the Poor Law Reform of 1834, were based upon inquiries of an empirical character which in care and completeness left little to be desired. But as a general rule Parliament has confined itself to accumulating information about the working of existing institutions; when an institution of a certain kind did not exist in this country, it has not created one for the purpose of trial, but has inquired into the working of such an institution in any foreign country where it happened to exist. This method is easy and inexpensive; nevertheless it involves a breach of Baconian rules; for analogy is much more remote and inference accordingly precarious between one country and another, as compared with one part and another of the same country.

Nor can it for a moment be contended that experiments have not been made and consciously described and treated as experiments. Robert Owen, for instance, established his mills and schools at New Lanark for the purpose of showing what might be done to elevate mill hands by wise and considerate treatment. He expressly described his establishment as *an experiment.* If not exactly the founder of the Factory Acts, he originated ideas and supplied practical evidence which was of the greatest value, so far as it could be appreciated at the time.

From time to time, too, statesmen have distinctly approved the experimental method. Thus, on 4th March 1835, Mr. Secretary Goulburn,[1] speaking of the new Factory Act of 1833, said that "he thought it the most expedient course to make an experiment of the law; so that from actual experience, rather than from contradictory opinions, they might be enabled to ascertain what alterations really were necessary." In the debate upon the second reading of the Factory and Workshop Bill (11th February 1878), Mr. Fielden, whose father was one of the leaders of the party which carried forward the improvement of the Factory Law, remarked that "in all its legislation upon the subject Parliament had been guided by experience, and had gradually extended the operations of the Acts from one trade to another." In the same debate the Home Secretary expressed his concurrence in the statement that such legislation proceeded on "a tentative system." It must be quite apparent too that the common practice of passing an Act and then remedying its mistakes, oversights, omitted cases, incon-

[1] Hansard's *Parliamentary Debates,* 3d Series, vol. xxvi. p. 527.

veniences, or unforeseen wrongs, in successive Amendment Acts, is really an application of the tentative or experimental method.

It ought also to be pointed out that the late Mr. Newmarch explained the empirical or experimental character of legislative method. Speaking at the British Association in 1861 he said: "From the plan suggested by the Statistical Congress of last year, they would gradually be able to ascertain what was the real condition, and what was the effect, of the social relations pervading different parts of the world. The application of the experimental method pursued during the last thirty years had led to a large modification of the early economic science in reference to free colonisation, legal interference with labour," etc. The idea that legislation is and must be essentially experiential, if not experimental, pervades this remarkable address, which is printed in full in the Journal of the Statistical Society for December 1861, vol. xxiv. p. 453, etc.

Legislative Experimentation.—But in order that we may pursue a truly Baconian course in legislation, we must not merely make experiments, but we must make them in the particular way calculated to prove or disprove the conclusion in view. There is manifest advantage, for instance, in making a legislative change in certain cities or districts only, so that we may observe what happens both where the change is in operation, and also in closely proximate places, where it is not in operation. This is often the only way in which we can clearly learn what is really the effect of the change in question; because if applied universally the effects of the new course will be merged into the general aggregate of many existing and varying effects. Nor is there usually any practical obstacle in the way of such partial trial. Since the article referred to was published, the Postmaster-General actually applied the experimental method in the introduction of the penny stamp savings bank forms. These forms were first tried by distribution in certain selected counties, and the results were inquired into before the measure was adopted generally. Although the case was not one suited to test the method effectively, the complete success of the trial tends distinctly in favour of experimental legislation.

It is not possible to repeat here all that was said in the article referred to in favour of direct appeal to experience. The fact, however, is, that the real difficulty will consist, not in making such appeals, but in knowing when to make them, how to interpret the results, and how far to depend upon our inferences. Experience must be our guide when we can enjoy such an advantage, but it is often the most difficult thing in the world to know what experience teaches. The palpable and direct result will often be the least part of the matter. A fence erected around machinery palpably saves people from falling among such machinery; but how are we to prove that it does not generate recklessness which will lead the people to fall into other dangers? We have to fall back upon vague presumptions and general inferences. An operative advocating a strike may easily point to other strikes in like circumstances which have benefited the strikers—to all appearance. Here are experiments to the point. It would require a great deal of inquiry and much argument of a vague kind to convince an economist that the striker really was benefited in the long-run.

It will now be apparent that the true method of approaching a legislative measure assumes the form of a complicated logical and scientific problem. It is granted, or at least assumed, that anything is right and expedient in legislation which adds to the sum of happiness of the community. But how to show this? It is not sufficient to show by direct experiment or other incontestable evidence that an addition of happiness is made. We must also assure ourselves that there is no equivalent or greater subtraction of happiness,—a subtraction which may take effect either as regards other people or subsequent times. This, it need hardly be said, is a more difficult matter. There is the difficulty of discovering and measuring, as Bastiat so clearly put it, "that which is not seen, as well as that which is seen." Let it, moreover, be clearly understood that in thus endeavouring to see the invisible we must make use of any science, or of all sciences which have any bearing upon the matter. It seems to be commonly supposed that certain matters are to be treated by economic science; others by moral science or jurisprudence; others, again, are questions of mere physical science only. It would generally be implied, for instance, that questions relating to corn or wages are purely economic; that marriage is a simply moral question; that the building of a bridge is one of engineering science or physics.

Relation of Science to Legislation.—The relation of science to social legislation will now become apparent. Each science is an aggregate of natural laws, more or less general; and these laws, when divested of metaphysical wrappings, resolve themselves into probabilities that certain consequences will follow from certain conjunctions of antecedents. Obviously, at whatever end the legislator aims, he must consult all those sciences whose probabilities bear upon this end. If, for instance, the matter under consideration be colliery explosions, supposed to arise from the firing of shots or blasts, there is —(1) the probability that the blasting is really the cause of the explosion; (2) the probability that more efficient ventilation would render the blasting harmless; (3) that if gunpowder were prohibited, compressed air or some other agent would be brought into successful operation; (4) that if blasting were confined to the night time, the mines could still be worked; and so forth, until we come finally to the probability that if the mines in question were actually thrown out of use, more harm than good would result. The legislator must look at such questions in an all-round manner. He is neither chemist, nor physicist, nor physician, nor economist, nor moralist, but all of these in some degree, and something more as well, in the sense that he must gather to a focus the complex calculus of probabilities, the data of which are supplied by the separate investigators. The Minister of State, as it is said, acts "upon advice." It is impossible that he should read up all the text-books of the sciences concerned, but he takes from the most reliable professors of each branch of science their inferences as bearing directly upon the matter. Here evidently we meet the reason why so few men of science are legislators, and so few legislators are men of science. The occupations are almost incompatible. The profound man of science must restrict his purview, whereas the legislator must be equally open to truth—that is to say, probability, from whatever quarter it comes. And although the legislator in matters of trade has perhaps more to do with economics than with any other science, yet on this very account he may need the more caution, lest he attribute exclusive value to the economic probabilities, and overlook moral, sanitary, political, and other probabilities.

Complications of the Subject.—After the preceding general remarks on the principles of legislation in matters of industry, we may proceed to consider how far certain of the more important or imminent questions may be treated on those principles. Industrial legislation is, indeed, of such extent and complication of detail that we cannot do more in the available space than select typical cases. The subject would be comparatively simple were we concerned only with the direct relations of the State to individuals. Even in this respect there is complication enough, when we remember the vast variety of trades which have to be considered, and the fourfold classes of persons to be legislated for in various degrees and manners—namely, men, women, young persons, and children.

In reality, however, the most difficult questions arise, not from the relations of the State to individuals, but from its relations to aggregates and organisations of individuals. After all, the State may perhaps be described, with a little pardonable hyperbole, as the least of the powers which govern us. Law is but the consecration of custom and public opinion. Whether in the home, the school, the workshop, or the public meeting, we are really governed by an indefinite amount of common law. More especially is this the case in the factory and the exchange. Men of the same trade cannot meet together without entering into some kind of combination, tending to govern its constituents and to affect the interests of outsiders. Industrial society is, and always has been, more or less honeycombed with cliques and corners and cabals, each with its own ideas of private interest, and its own code of right and wrong. As we shall presently see, trade societies or guilds are among the oldest institutions of which we have any historical information, and they doubtless existed long before their existence came to be recorded.

The relation of the State to labour is a question not so much of the direct restraint of the labourer by the State, as of the manner in which the State can regard the voluntary and unauthorised legislation of the labourers themselves. It may be that the work of the State will consist in increasing rather than lessening the liberty of the individual workman. In any case, it is impossible to treat of industrial legislation without fully taking into account the rules and restraints under which labour exists. We shall, however, best approach the difficulties of the subject by considering, in the first place, the modes and degrees in which it is expedient for the State to control labour directly. We shall then have some clue to the question, how far individuals are justified in attempting to control their fellow-workmen. Next there arises the higher question, how far the State ought to control individuals in their attempts at controlling each other. Even when we can clearly perceive that the action of a "corner" or a trades union is pernicious, it does not necessarily follow that the State would do well to intervene. In some cases evils are best left to work their own remedy; in other cases attempted intervention would only aggravate the evil. There are often, moreover, several ways of approaching the same end: in some cases an institution may need to be summarily suppressed; in other cases it may be allowed to show its own worthlessness and futility; in yet other cases rival institutions may be set up to undermine and counteract that which is deemed pernicious; occasionally, instead of trying to suppress the obnoxious institution, it may be favoured and promoted, in the hope that the good which is in it may grow and the evil die away; nor is this at all an exhaustive statement of the many indirect ways in which legislation may be brought to bear upon an industrial problem. Not uncommonly we may hesitate between the several ways, and perhaps wait for further experience to indicate the best method of setting to work. If we only have carefully-recorded information about it, every institution may be regarded as an experiment tending to show its own success or non-success.

CHAPTER II

DIRECT INTERFERENCE OF THE STATE WITH LABOUR

THE manner, occasion, and degree in which the State may interfere with the industrial freedom of its citizens is one of the most debatable and difficult questions of social science. Existing legislation, which all allow to be necessary, obliges us on the one hand to look upon such interference as justifiable in certain circumstances; more general considerations lead us to look upon freedom as the normal state. There is a wide intervening tract, where the line of demarcation is very differently drawn by different thinkers. The question arises, moreover, whether the matter is not one which must be decided according to circumstance of time, place, history, and national character.

It might perhaps be expected that we could learn a good deal about labour legislation from the English Statute-Book, which now covers in almost unbroken continuity an interval of 650 years. There is no want of such legislation in that great book; in fact, there is over-abundance, and we may learn something from the failure and futility of much that has been enacted by English Parliaments. But the great lesson which we learn, and it is an impressive one, is that legislation with regard to labour has almost always been class-legislation. It is the effort of some dominant body to keep down a lower class, which had begun to show inconvenient aspirations. Such is clearly the nature of the celebrated Statute of Labourers, which was simply a futile attempt to prevent labour from getting its proper price. Brentano is doubtless right in saying that all statutes of labourers in the Middle Ages were framed with regard to the powers and wants of the landed proprietors, the feudal lords. The great Statute of Apprentices (5 Eliz. cap. 4), of which I shall have much to say, had a different origin. According to the opinion of historians, it represented the triumph of the craft-guilds—that is, the mediæval trade-unions. If it was this, it was also more than this. Regarded as a piece of legislative handiwork, it certainly left nothing to be desired in thoroughness and comprehensiveness; but it was nevertheless a monstrous law. From beginning to end it aimed at industrial slavery. The Justices of the Peace could not only fix all rates of wages, but if they chose to exert their powers, could become the industrial despots of their district.

It has often been weakly remarked that probably this statute, however indefensible it may seem at the present day, was well suited to the then existing state of society. Such remarks imply ignorance of the contents of the statute. The general theory of the Act is that every servant or artificer shall be compelled to work in the trade to which he was brought up. Any workman departing from his city, town, or parish, without a testimonial from his previous employer or some officer, was to be imprisoned until he procured a testimonial; or if he could not do so within the space of one and twenty days, was to be whipped and used as a vagabond. The hours of labour were prescribed, not, as in our Factory Acts, by way of limitation, but by imposition. Thus, from the middle of the month of March to the middle of September all artificers and labourers hired by time were to be and continue at their work at or before five o'clock in the morning, and continue at work and not depart until betwixt seven and eight of the clock at night—two and a half hours in the course of the day being allowed for meals and drinking. Thus the legal day's work was to be about twelve hours *at the least.*

As to young women, they were simply at the orders of the magistrates; for the 24th section enacts that any two Justices of the Peace or other competent magistrates shall "appoint any such woman as is of the age of twelve years and under the age of forty years and unmarried, and forth of service, as they shall think meet to serve, to be retained or serve by the year, or by the week or day, for such wages and in such reasonable sort and manner as they shall think meet; and if any such woman shall refuse so to serve, then it shall be lawful for the said Justices of Peace, Mayor, or Head Officers, to commit such woman to ward, until she shall be bounden to serve as is aforesaid." Lest the Justices should be lax in regulating the service of labourers, they were to be paid for their trouble. Such was liberty—such was industry under "good Queen Bess,"—at least such it was in the Statute-Book, and in the intention of the governing classes. In operation the statute was, there is reason to believe, little more than a dead letter, except as regards the important sections relating to apprenticeship, of which the evil influence has hardly yet died out. It has often been boasted that the laws of England were always just and equal to all classes; this may be true of much judge-made law, but it is decisively contradicted by such a monstrous statute, from the operation of which the higher classes and even their servants were expressly exempted. Yet this Statute of Apprentices was not finally and completely repealed until six years ago by the Conspiracy and Protection of Property Act (38 and 39 Vict. cap. 86, sec. 17, III. *a*).

An Old Experiment in Industrial Legislation.—In many cases we learn from the preamble or other contents of a statute regulating a trade that it was really passed at the instance of the trade for their supposed advantage. This is most plain in the case of the Act touching drapers, cottoners, and frizers of Shrewsbury (8 Eliz. cap. 7), which commences by reciting that there has been in Shrewsbury time out of mind of man a guild of the art and mystery of drapers lawfully incorporated. This guild, it appeared, was used most commonly to set on work above six hundred persons of the art or science of shearmen or frizers. Divers artificers and other persons of Shrewsbury, however, not being of the said company or mystery, "nor brought up in the use of the said trade, have of late with great disorder, upon a mere covetous desire and mind, intromitted with and occupied the said trade of buying Welsh cloth or lining, having no knowledge, experience, or skill in the same." After further describing the dire evils thus produced by successful competition, the Act proceeds to prohibit every person inhabiting in Shrewsbury from occupying the trade of buying Welsh cottons, etc., unless he be free thereof. However quaintly and candidly expressed, there is nothing in this statute but the simple spirit of trade monopoly. We may wonder indeed that the cottoners of Shrewsbury could so easily move the great statesmen of Queen Elizabeth in their favour; but the policy of the cottoners was of a piece with the policy of Lord Burleigh, as so strikingly formulated in the Statute of Apprentices above referred to. What, however, is very strange about the Shrewsbury cottoners is that before six years were over they had not only found out their error, but candidly confessed it to the powers. In the Act 14 Eliz. cap. 12, we find the previous Act almost entirely repealed, "at the humble suit of the inhabitants of the said town, and also of the said artificers, for whose benefit the said Act was supposed to be provided." Nor is this all; for in the second section the moral of the matter is brought out in the clearest terms. "Experience hath plainly taught in the said town that the said Act hath not only not brought the good effect that then was hoped and surmised, but also hath been and now is likely to be the very greatest cause of the impoverishing and undoing of the poor artificers and others, at whose suit the said Act was procured, for that there be now, sithence the making of the said statute, much fewer persons to set them a-work than before," etc. etc. Were it not that the Lord Chancellor Bacon was then a boy of only eleven years of age, we might have thought that he had had a hand in drawing this Act, where the value of experience is brought out in so truly a Baconian manner.

Parliament, since the 14th year of Elizabeth, has made many great mistakes and failures, and has had often to eat its own words. But it has seldom taken the lessons of experience in the same spirit of candour and philosophy.

The Common Law.—We ought not, however, to forget that, in England at least, the statute-book contains but half the law. The unwritten and judge-made common law has always held a very different tone in matters of industry. The same judges who delighted themselves with the intricacies of the law of real estate held one simple rule about industry—that it should be free. It would be very difficult to say when this doctrine of the common law took its rise. As Blackstone said of the common law in general, its rise is like that of the Nile—unknown. Some persons have found the principle of non-restraint of trade in the Great Charter; but Article 41 of that charter (re-enacted by 2 Edw. III. cap. 9) only refers to foreign merchants trading in England. There is no reference to the general industry of the people, who, it need hardly be said, were by no means free at that time. It seems likely that the extremely wise course of the judges was due in no small degree to natural reaction against the tyranny of the statute law, the greed of class legislators, and the illegal encroachments of the Crown. The judges were the only disinterested parties in power, and however they might delight on other occasions to display their acumen in logical quibbles, they took in trade questions the interest of the whole community as their sole guide. In this course they were much assisted by the fact that the

Statute of Apprentices, when enacting in the 31st section that none may use any manual occupation except he hath been apprentice to the same, fortunately confined this restriction to "any craft, mystery, or occupation now used or occupied within the realm." The words "now used or occupied" were inserted, I presume, from regard to the logical impossibility of any new trade springing up, if its "occupiers" were required to have passed through a seven years' apprenticeship before occupying it. Lord Burleigh, or the other ingenious authors of the statute, not foreseeing the development of modern industry, made no attempt to circumvent this difficulty, and the fortunate result was that all the new industries of the seventeenth and eighteenth centuries were left to free development. The Act contained the elements of its own abrogation.

Government Inspection of Commodities.—To illustrate these views of the proper limits of legislative action we cannot do better than consider the reasons which may be urged for and against the system of submitting commodities to the scrutiny of Government officers. Herrings are branded by Government inspectors in Scotland; kegs of butter are tested and weighed in some Irish markets. Gun-barrels are proved in Birmingham; gold and silver plate must be marked at the Assay Offices; meat and fish are inspected by sanitary officers; public analysts are appointed to detect the adulteration of groceries, drugs, and some kinds of food. Are not all these cases violations of the general principle that the individual is the best judge of his own needs and interests? On what principle, if any, are these particular classes of things submitted to an arbitrary system of State supervision, while the far greater number and bulk of commodities are left to the great principle of *laisser faire?*

It may well be said, on the one hand, that laws defining what we shall wear and eat,—sumptuary laws, as they have been called,—were long since repealed by general consent. Statutes of Edward III., Edward IV., and Henry VIII. prescribed minute regulations about peaked shoes, short doublets, and long coats. They were all repealed as long ago as the first year of James I. (cap. 25). Are we gradually to get back to a somewhat similar system in which the articles which we use must be passed by a Government officer before we are allowed to buy and use them? By degrees inspectors will make their way into our houses to see that our drains are in good order, our rooms well ventilated, our kitchen boilers safe, our cisterns clean, our children at school.

If this sort of thing is to progress, we shall be guided and tutored and inspected at every hour of the day.

But in discussing these matters we need above all things *discrimination.* One hundred modes of Government interference might be mentioned, of which fifty might be very desirable and fifty condemnable. In each case, as I contend, we must look to the peculiar aim, purpose, means, and circumstances of the case. Sumptuary laws, for instance, bear no analogy to recent sanitary laws. They were mere class laws, intended to support the pride of an aristocracy by restraining the tastes of the lower classes. If any pretext was put forward about saving the purses of the poor, and preventing them from running into extravagance, it was a too obvious pretence. The roots of the legislation of this kind were in pride and oppression.

The purpose of recent Government interference in trade is widely different. Whether that interference is wise or not we will presently consider; but those who examine such things as herrings, butter, gun-barrels, coffee, tea, pepper, butchers'-meat, and the like, cannot be charged with indifference or opposition to the good of the common people. But why examine and certify these and a few other things, and leave the great mass of commodities—chairs and tables, hats, shoes, calicoes, woollen cloths, and so on *ad infinitum*—to the unfettered choice of the purchaser? Discrimination is here again needed.

It ought to be easily seen that commodities fall into two distinct categories, according as the purchaser is or is not the best judge of what he wants. The pattern of a dress, the style of a bonnet, the shape of a pair of boots, the tone of a picture, the melody of a piece of music, are matters in which the intending purchaser is necessarily the final judge, at least for the time being. If the pattern of a dress is pleasing to the intending wearer, that settles the matter; no Government inspector can make it unpleasing. The question is one of taste and individual preference. Now the greater number of commodities fall into this category: whether we are buying books or pictures, or horses or carriages, a mansion or an estate, or anything ministering to our personal feelings, we are clearly the best judges. Similarly, the palatableness of drinking water, the flavour of wine, the pungency of pepper, are matters of which every consumer may be supposed able to judge.

But it is a totally different question whether a purchaser in certain cases knows what he is buying. A man, for instance, about to buy a mansion tries the water out of the well, and is satisfied by its sparkling limpidity and its brisk taste. A chemist would have pointed out that these are suspicious symptoms, and analysis might have detected deadly sewage poison. The drains of a mansion, again, are a different matter from its style of architecture, or the view from its windows. It is a pure matter of technical skill to say whether the existing drains ensure freedom from infectious sewer gases. A sanitary inspector can decide this with indefinitely greater approach to certainty than the average householder. In a similar way it may be easily allowed that he who can judge the pungency of cayenne pepper cannot by taste detect the red lead which colours it. He who selects the greenest pickles may be unaware of the copper which gives the attractive tinge.

It must surely be allowed, then, that there are many cases where the expert is a far better judge than the individual purchaser. Common sense would in these cases, of course, lead us to desire the opinion of the expert before purchasing. We might, it is true, still leave the matter to individual action. A whole profession of food analysts would spring into existence if the ordinary paterfamilias made a rule of sending samples of his grocer's supplies to be examined. *Laisser faire* policy might still be maintained if everybody understood his interests. But the very point of the matter is that ignorant people cannot take precautions against dangers of which they are ignorant. While it is a fact that people live in badly-drained houses, drink sewage water, purchase bad meat or adulterated groceries, it is of no use urging that their interests would lead them not to do so. The fact demolishes any amount of presumption and argument. The same considerations apply to various other cases, such as the testing of gun-barrels, the assay of plate, and the like. Nobody can possibly wish to be blown up when shooting off a rifle or fowling-piece; but no purchaser, by mere visual examination, can tell that an apparently sound and beautifully-constructed barrel is really safe.

It must surely be apparent that in such cases the Government officer who steps in and prevents the faulty article from being exposed to sale does not really restrict the liberty of the purchaser. We may assume that no consumer wants to buy putrid sausages, poisonous pickles, dangerous guns, or fraudulent plate. Thus the Government official who excludes these things from public sale actually assists the purchaser in carrying out his own desires. We come, therefore, to the view long since maintained by the great economist Jean-Baptiste Say, that Government may properly interfere to prevent abuses in those special cases where it is impossible, or at least difficult, for the buyer of goods to verify their character for himself. (See the *Catéchisme d'Economie Politique*, chap. xxi. *Cours*, 4me *Partie*, chap. x. vol. iii. p. 278 *seq.*)

Multiplication of Efficiency of the Expert.—It can hardly fail to be noticed, too, that an immense increase of efficiency and multiplication of utility is secured by appointing officers to assist and protect the public in certain special points. The whole division and subdivision of labour is but a case of Mr. Herbert Spencer's doctrine of evolution, and the evolution of special Government inspectors is a case of division of labour. It is obviously impossible that an ordinary person busily engaged in his ordinary daily occupation can acquire the technical knowledge and skill requisite to enable him to test the purity of the groceries, water, milk, meat, ale, gas, and other commodities daily consumed in his house. If he does attempt to acquire the knowledge, and provide himself with the requisite apparatus for testing, how needlessly great is the trouble and expense, considering that a single officer, provided with one set of apparatus, may do the work for a whole town. However zealous and clever the individual may be, he cannot compete in skill with an officer devoted to the occupation, who, besides giving his whole time and thought to the work, has opportunities of varied experience and comparison. An individual householder, for instance, can inspect his own drains and those of a few friends. But an authorised sanitary inspector may go from house to house all over the parish or district. He sees drains of all kinds—good, bad, and indifferent. He learns by repeated observation where evil is likely to arise, and by what change it can be avoided. He enjoys, in fact, all the resources of experience and experiment. The same advantages are enjoyed by every inspector whose business it is to pass from factory to factory, from school to school, from shop to shop, and who sees what is good and bad in each place.

It is no slight further advantage in favour of Government action that an inspector becomes acquainted with the law and legal procedure applying to his business, and can put the law in operation with immensely greater ease and efficiency than can a private person. We might think, for instance, that everybody would take care to get full weight when they buy a sack of coals, a pound of sugar, or an ounce of tobacco. The law provides the fullest remedies and penalties for giving short weight; and in the special cases of coals and bread it obliges the deliverer to carry scales and weights to the purchaser's house, in order that he may weigh them on the spot if so minded. But experience proves that private persons seldom test the weights of commodities they buy, and probably never prosecute those who use false scales and weights. The reasons are sufficiently obvious. The loss of time involved in a prosecution is almost sufficient reason, without taking into account the cost, the obloquy, and the chance of making some mistake which will turn the tables against the prosecutor. But a single official inspector of weights and measures can do for a whole town what they cannot do for themselves. Without personal offence, and as a mere matter of routine, he tests all scales and weights; he knows precisely when and how to prosecute, and can conduct a number of prosecutions at the same time. Everything is in his favour.

It seems to be certain, again, that a skilled inspector can detect dangerous high-pressure boilers incomparably better than persons not specially expert in the matter. The advantage of some system of Government inspection cannot be seriously denied, and the only question which remains is, whether the inspection should be directly governed from Whitehall, or should be indirectly carried on through local bodies of experts.

The Herring-Brand System.—Although it seems impossible to hold that Government inspection of retail food supplies is inexpedient, a very different question is raised in the case of the herring-brand system in Scotland, or the tasting and sizing of butter kegs in Ireland. Such regulation affects the wholesale trade, and is, in fact, chiefly brought into action as regards goods intended for exportation. The inspection and branding is not compulsory, as it formerly was, but is largely used by producers, owing to the facility with which barrels of herrings or butter thus branded are accepted in foreign markets. Branded barrels of herrings are, in fact, endowed with the property of currency—that is to say, they pass from owner to owner without sampling or examination of any kind. They can be ordered, bought, sold, or assigned as security for advances, by the mere specifying of the crown brand.

There can be no question that this system is nearly, if not quite, anomalous. Its only analogues are found in the Hall marking of gold and silver plate and jewellery, in the proving of gun-barrels, or in the coining of the Queen's money at the mint. Of the two former cases it may be said that they are compulsory regulations required to prevent fraud or accident. Of money it may be said that, although a commodity, it is a very peculiar one. The herring-brand cannot possibly be said to be necessary, for sundry large herring-curers dispense with the stamp of the State, and argue that they can sell their produce at a somewhat better price without it. Still the great bulk of the curers are not of this opinion, when we find that in a recent season 660,000 barrels of herrings, cured by perhaps

400 different curers, were examined and branded, this work being accomplished by only twenty-six official inspectors. The great opponent of the system was that doctrinaire-economist, MacCulloch, who, in his well-known Commercial Dictionary, advocated the complete abolition of the Fishery Board of Scotland. The inspection, he held, was in point of fact utterly useless. It was an attempt on the part of Government to do that for their subjects which they could do far better for themselves. If the official inspection were put an end to, merchants and others who buy herrings would themselves inspect the barrels; and while any attempt at fraud would thus be effectually obviated, curers could prepare their herrings in any way they pleased without being compelled to prepare fish in the same way for the tables of the poor as for those of the rich. Then, having denounced the system as useless, MacCulloch proceeds in his characteristic way to discover that it is far worse than useless, being, "rather a security against the detection of fraud, than against its existence." The immense expansion of the herring trade since the date of MacCulloch's remarks (1840), and the general use of the brand to the present day, is the answer which experience gives. It is impossible that the brand should still carry the Scotch cured herring through all parts of the world were it the mere cloak for deception which was asserted.

MacCulloch's theoretical objections and the discontent of some members of the trade led, however, in 1848, to the despatch of a Treasury Commissioner, who was to inquire into the expenditure and operations of the Scotch Fishery Board. This duty was entrusted to the late John George Shaw Lefevre, and the result was a most able, and to my mind conclusive, report on the subject, reprinted in John M. Mitchell's excellent work on *The Herring* (Edinburgh, 1864). The commissioner went with no leaning towards the system, but came back impressed with its usefulness. The only serious objection to the system which he admits is, that it somewhat tends to discourage the improvements of private enterprise by promoting a uniform limit of price which it is difficult to pass. The Government brand indeed is purely optional; yet so long as the great majority of the trade adopt it, other curers find great difficulty in dispensing with it. On the other hand, the trade generally uphold the system as facilitating trade in herrings, and preventing disputes or repudiation of orders. Lefevre summed up the results of his inquiry in these words: "I feel compelled, notwithstanding the objection in principle to which it is liable, to recommend that it should still be maintained." He suggested, indeed, that a small fee should be imposed to meet the expenses of the Fishery Board, and this suggestion was carried into effect in 1859, fourpence being charged for each barrel branded. So much, however, has the use of the brand extended, that the fees for 1880 were estimated at £11,000, or about £7000 beyond the whole expenses of the branding staff.

Here we are brought to a very interesting dilemma in industrial legislation. Experience decisively confirms the advantages of a system which is in conflict with principle, at least in the estimation of MacCulloch, Lefevre, and many other economists.

There are, indeed, many cases of commodities of which the purchaser can be no good judge, but which the

Legislature has never thought of certifying. No ordinary person, for instance, can possibly judge the quality of a watch which, from all that appears to the unpractised eye, might be worth £10 or £50. Nevertheless, it is out of the question that Government officers should be employed to inspect and stamp watches before they are allowed to be exposed for sale. The sufficient reason is, no doubt, that watches differ infinitely in details of construction and finish, so that it would be impossible to say exactly what the certification meant, or how long it would hold good. The fineness of the gold or silver composing the case is a simple definite fact which can be tested in a few moments and exactly recorded.

From a review of what precedes we may perhaps infer that Government branding is only to be approved under the following joint conditions—(1) When some special danger is to be avoided, or some special considerable advantage to be attained by Government intervention; (2) When the individual is not able to exercise proper judgment and supervision on his own behalf; (3) When the intervention required is of a simple and certain character, and the result can be certified in a manner comprehensible to all.

Ancient Sanitary and Trade Regulations.—It is well worthy of notice that the tendency towards sanitary inspection which some people now dread as an approach to despotism, is in reality a very old institution. A study of Riley's translation of the *Liber Albus*, or "White Book of the City of London," and a glance through Mr. G. L. Gomme's *Index of Municipal Offices* (Index Society), will show that the ancient municipalities of this land were minutely organised in this respect. Ale-conners, ale-founders, ale-tasters, auditors, aulnegers, beadles, bread-weighers, coal-meters, flesh-searchers, and inspectors and searchers under various other names, were employed by our ancestors to save themselves from unapparent frauds and evils. I think, too, that Mr. Gomme has clearly shown, in other writings, that the municipalities were no creations of Norman monarchs, but were really developments of original village communities. So far, therefore, as antiquarian learning can go, we have the fullest warrant for the functions of Government objected to by some persons. The tendency to centralisation, again, which is involved in much recent legislation, is due partly to the decay of local activity, and partly to the immense improvements in communication, which render every part of a kingdom now almost as accessible to the seat of government as were the outlying parts of an extensive parish or hundred to its local lords in early days. It is the vastly greater scale on which our legislative operations now proceed which makes them bear the appearance of offensive innovations and despotic encroachments.

In former days, too, much trouble was taken by the Government to ensure the excellence of several kinds of goods, especially woollen cloth. The Act 2d and 3d Philip and Mary, cap. 12, for instance, provides for the viewing and sealing of clothes called Bridgwaters. At Leeds the ancient regulations of the Cloth Hall continued to be exercised in full vigour until about the middle of last century. The fact, however, is, that the old system of Government certification has been replaced within the last hundred years by the modern system of trade-marks, the legislation of which, however, is only now being carried into effect under the Trade-Mark Acts of 1875 and 1876. The trade-mark or trade-name is a private brand, and it is essential to the continued success of a firm that they shall uphold the reputation of their marks by carefully supervising the qualities of the goods to which they are affixed. Registered trade-marks being now legal property, manufacturers become their own branders, and are urged to brand honestly by the powerful and constantly-acting motive of self-interest. Both statute and judge-made law have of late tended strongly to create and maintain property in trade reputation, and the effect is probably very good. But I see nothing in this to prohibit the employment of State inspection and certification in cases where it can be clearly shown to possess superior advantages.

As frequent complaints are now made in the manufacturing districts as to frauds committed in the packing of cotton,—earth, stones, brick-bats, and rubbish of all descriptions being sometimes found inside the bales,—it may be pointed out that such matters were well looked after by our ancestors. The packing of wool was superintended by a special officer qualified and admitted before the mayor and constables of the staple of Westminster. An elaborate treaty of commerce between Henry VII. and the Duke of Burgundy, contracted in the year 1499, provided that all wool exported should be packed by duly qualified packers, who were to certify by labels the quality of the wool. Penalties were enacted against any fraud, cheat, collusion, or deceit, especially against those who should "pack or fold up earth, stones, dung, sand, gravel, or hair in the fleeces."

CHAPTER III

THE FACTORY ACTS AND SIMILAR LEGISLATION DIRECTLY AFFECTING LABOURERS

THE most important mass of legislative enactments relating to labour is contained in the Factory Acts, now consolidated into the very important, long, and complicated statute known as the Factory and Workshop Act, 1878 (41 Vict. cap. 16). This Act, mainly due, as regards the passing, to Mr. (now Sir) Assheton Cross, forms a complete code of factory regulations, and replaces about sixteen previous statutes, which are enumerated and repealed in a schedule. There can be no doubt that, whether we look to the several more tentative acts by which this was preceded, to the inquiries connected with them, to the diligent and zealous labours of the factory inspectors, to the thorough inquiries of the Factory Act Commissioners of 1875,—conducted to no small extent by personal examination of the workshops,—or finally, to the prolonged and exhaustive debates in committee of the House of Commons, by which the details of the Act were finally settled,—this Consolidation Act is one of the brightest achievements of legislation in this or any other country. The great fact is that it embodies disinterested legislation: the health and welfare of the people at large form the sole object; no one class or trade is to be promoted, as in almost all the older industrial laws. If anything, it involves a sacrifice on the part of those capitalists and employers who were greatly concerned in passing it. Before, however, entering further into the matter of existing factory legislation, it will be well to consider as briefly as possible the course of events which have led up to the present state of the law.

History of English Factory Legislation.—Not only is it impossible to attempt anything approaching to a history of factory legislation, but it is also unnecessary. The report or essay upon this subject prepared by Ernst, Edler von Plener, the first Secretary of the Austro-Hungarian embassy in London, leaves nothing to be desired as a most clear, accurate, and compendious historical sketch of the subject. It has been excellently translated into English by F. L. Weinmann, and published with an Introduction by Mr. Mundella (London, Chapman and Hall, 1873). This convenient little book contains also, as an appendix, abstracts of Continental laws and regulations respecting the labour and education of children employed in factories. The history of factory legislation is not only highly technical, involving details of hours and arrangements of little general interest, but it is also complicated by the intrusion of political intrigues and struggles.

The first of the Factory Acts was the so-called Health and Morals Act, passed in 1802 (42 Geo. III. cap. 73), and generally known as the Elder Sir Robert Peel's Act. It appears to have originated out of the practice of apprenticeship—many children having been sent by the poor-law overseers of the southern counties, under bonds of apprenticeship, to the rising manufacturing towns of the north. These children were treated hardly better than slaves, which indeed they really were. They were worked day and night, and it is even said that one gang, when exhausted, went to rest in the beds still warm of those who were coming on to work. Attention having been drawn to this state of things by the epidemics which arose from overcrowding, a Board of Health was appointed in 1796, and in 1802 the Act already named was passed, which declares in the preamble that certain regulations were become necessary to preserve the health and morals of the great number of male and female apprentices whom it was then the practice to employ in cotton and woollen mills. The Act began by requiring factories to be well whitewashed twice a year, and a sufficient number of windows to be provided to supply fresh air. The next clause obliges every master to supply each of his apprentices with one new suit of clothes yearly, showing that it was legally bound apprentices with whom the Act really dealt. The time of working was not to exceed twelve hours daily, and night work was prohibited, with certain exceptions. Apprentices were to be instructed in reading, writing, and arithmetic. Male and female apprentices were not to sleep in the same room, nor were more than two to sleep in the same bed. A long clause governs the instruction and conduct of apprentices on Sundays, all these matters being looked after by two visitors appointed by the justices. The point of greatest interest about this Act, now wholly repealed by the Factory and Workshop Act, is the fact that it applied directly only to legal apprentices, who, being industrial slaves, indubitably needed the protection of the law. Thus was the thin end of the wedge introduced.

In course of time, however, it was brought to the notice of Parliament that great numbers of children residing near factories were being worked in an excessive and injurious manner, because they did not enjoy the protection of the Act described. As the evils produced were practically as great as if the children had been legal apprentices, the parents being almost as grasping and careless of the children's health as the masters, Parliament could not deny the need of inquiry. The evidence given before a Select Committee of the House of Commons in 1816 led to the passing in 1819 of the Second Factory Act (59 Geo. III. cap. 66), which applied, however, only to cotton mills. The age at which children could be admitted to such mills was now for the first time limited to nine years of age or upwards. Between the ages of nine and sixteen the hours of labour were not to exceed twelve per day, exclusive of meal times, and night work was again prohibited. Some trifling exceptions were allowed in the case of water mills, which suffer from irregularity of water-power, such exceptions existing even in the present day.

Progress was again made in 1825 by an Act passed by Sir John Cam Hobhouse (6 Geo. IV. cap. 63), which, besides a more thorough restriction of labour as regards children under sixteen years, introduced a half or rather quarter holiday on Saturdays. The work on that day was not to exceed nine hours in length, to be completed between five in the morning and half-past four in the afternoon. Meal hours were carefully provided, and labour of any kind during such hours absolutely prohibited. A register of children employed was now first required, and the signature of the parents or guardians of a child to the statement of age was to exempt employers from penalty in case of falsity. Powers were given or confirmed to justices, but the important provision was introduced that no justice being the proprietor or master of a cotton mill, or the father or son of such, should act as justice in respect of this law.

There soon followed that troublous time when trades unions were rampant and the Reform Bill imminent. The Factory king, Richard Oastler, now came forth into notoriety, advocating a Ten Hours Bill. The only immediate fruit of the agitation, however, was the Act 1 and 2 Will. IV. cap. 39, which, while repealing five previous enactments, consolidated and slightly improved their provisions. But this Act had the great advantage of being carried into effect to a considerable extent, the law having been previously much disregarded. There soon followed, however, Lord Althorp's Act of 1833 (3 and 4 Will. IV. cap. 103), which introduced several important novelties. The distinction was now introduced, which has been ever since maintained, between "children" admitted to work of the ages nine to thirteen years, and "young persons" of ages from thirteen to eighteen years. The attendance of children at school was now also rendered compulsory, and effectively provided for. Children were not to work more than nine hours per day, and were to spend two more hours daily in school. It is said that this "half-time" principle was quite accidentally discovered. Some means being sought whereby evidence should be available that a child was not working at a certain hour, it was suggested by Mr.

Edwin Chadwick that presence in school would afford the best possible evidence. Thus it came about that all factory children have for half a century past received something to call education.

Passing over many technical difficulties which were encountered in ascertaining the ages of children, whether by reference to stature, general appearance, dentition, etc., we come to the Consolidating Act, which Sir Robert Peel carried in 1844, namely the Factory Act (7 and 8 Vict. cap. 15). The hours of labour of children of eight (instead of nine) years of age and upwards were now reduced to six and a half, three hours' daily attendance at school for five days per week being further required. In some cases, however, alternate days of ten hours' labour and five hours' schooling were allowed. Various careful regulations were made about meal times, during which times no children nor young persons were to be allowed to remain in the workrooms. Many such regulations, which appear at first sight needless or oppressive, were found by experience to be requisite to prevent evasion of the law, and to facilitate discovery of infractions by the inspectors and sub-inspectors, who were now endowed with considerable powers. Under the original Health and Morals Act visitors were to be appointed by the local justices, but the law was generally disregarded. The Act of 1833 introduced the principle of centralisation, enabling the Crown to appoint four inspectors, with all kinds of functions, including, at that time, magisterial powers. The latter powers were retrenched by the Act of 1844, and inspectors must now prosecute before a court of summary jurisdiction; but in every other respect the inspectors have retained or advanced their functions, and they have been the key to the success of the whole system.

The subsequent Factory Acts are of less general interest, being chiefly occupied either with more narrowly defining hours, or with extending the provisions of the Acts to additional branches of industry. Thus the 13 and 14 Vict. cap. 54, defined the legal working day as limited between six in the morning and six in the evening, with an hour and a half for meals, leaving a maximum of ten and a half hours for work. Any person simply found upon the premises of a factory was to be deemed at work. A Saturday half-holiday after two o'clock was securely provided for.

The legislation so far described related only to textile factories—cotton, woollen, silk, or linen. Bleaching and dyeing works were only brought under restriction in 1860, by the 23 and 24 Vict. cap. 78. Mining industry had been regulated so far back as 1842, when the Mining Act (5 and 6 Vict. cap. 99) absolutely prohibited the employment of females, and boys under ten years of age, underground. In 1850 the supervision of mines was vastly improved by the Coal and Iron Mines Act (23 and 24 Vict. cap. 151) which introduced a variety of precautions as regards the health and safety of miners, and empowered the appointment of a staff of inspectors. In 1862 double shafts were required to be provided to coal mines. Several minor industries, such as manufactories of earthenware, lucifer matches, cartridges, etc., were brought under regulation in 1864.

A great advance was carried out by the Factory Acts Extension Act and the Workshop Regulation Act, both passed in 1867 (30 and 31 Vict. caps. 103 and 146), which brought almost all establishments to be called manufactories under supervision, the number of sub-inspectors being increased for the purpose. The regulations of the Workshop Act, however, were to be enforced by the local authorities. A kind of *experimentum crucis* was thus afforded to show the comparative merits of localised and centralised management, which resulted entirely in favour of the latter. Many town councils explicitly resolved not to interfere with trade, and many more silently ignored the Act, so that the inspectors were obliged to declare, in 1868 and 1869, that the Workshop Act was a dead letter. Comparatively little interest attaches to some of the subsequent Acts, such as that of 1870, extending the Factory Acts Extension Act to print, bleaching, and dyeing-works, and to preserving and fish-curing establishments, or the Amendment Act of 1871, allowing Jews to work on Sundays. Another Act of 1871 (34 and 35 Vict. cap. 104) transferred the supervision of workshops from the local authorities to the inspectors and sub-inspectors of factories, who were to enforce the law and make reports as in the case of factories. The Factories (Health of Women) Act of 1874 much enlarged the powers of inspectors, and made many small improvements in the law which it is needless to refer to, inasmuch as the whole of the laws relating to factories and workshops generally are consolidated and codified, as already stated, in the Act of 1878. The changes effected by this Act, indeed, were not great, the chief purpose of the consolidation being to make the law clear, consistent, and embodied in a single convenient code.

The Factory and Workshop Act, 1878.—This Act (41 Vict. cap. 16), which has no preamble at all, consists, in addition to two preliminary sections giving the short title and commencement of Act, of four principal parts, and six schedules. The first part contains the general law relating to factories and workshops, treating in succession of sanitary provisions, the safety of employees, their employment and meal hours, holidays, the education of children, certificates of fitness, and notice and investigation of accidents. Part II. is of a more detailed character, and provides specially for particular classes of factories and workshops as regards health and safety, special restrictions of employment, special exceptions regarding Jews, meal hours, overtime, night-work, domestic employment, etc. In Part III. the machinery of administration is provided—the appointment of inspectors, certifying surgeons, regulation of clocks, provision of registers, enforcement of penalties, and legal procedure, being provided for. There yet remains Part IV., which settles the difficult question of definition of terms, the mode of application of the Act to Scotland and Ireland, and adds a few trifling exceptions, finally repealing all the previous sixteen Factory Acts, and a few sections of other Acts, as enumerated in the sixth schedule. There are, moreover, five important schedules, giving detailed lists of occupations subject to certain special restrictions or exceptions. Such, however, are the complications of this remarkable code of law,—the mere table of contents filling eight pages and the text sixty-five,—that anything approaching to a commentary upon its effects would fill a large volume. In addition to several publications of Mr. Alexander Redgrave, a textbook of the Act has been published by Mr. G. J. Notcutt, entitled "The Law relating to Factories and Workshops, with Introduction and Explanatory Notes; comprising the Factory and Workshop Act, 1878, and the Orders of the Secretary of State made thereunder." Second Edition. London, 1879 (Stevens).

It is a peculiarly difficult task to give in a few words the general effect of this Act, because there are in almost every clause various alternatives or options in addition to exceptions and other complications. Thus every abbreviated statement is of necessity more or less inaccurate. The general assumption of the Act is, that labour in textile factories involves a more severe strain than that in non-textile factories and workshops. While the longest period for which a young person or woman may be employed in textile labour without an interval for meals is four and a half hours, the corresponding limit for other labour is five hours. Textile factories are defined in section 93 as premises in which steam, water, or other mechanical power is used in manufacturing cotton, wool, hair, silk, flax, etc., not including bleach, print, and various other kinds of works. Non-textile factories are described in a long schedule; and workshops are practically any places not being factories where manufacture is carried on.

The hours of work seem to be in no case absolutely fixed, but on five days a week are either to begin not before 6 A.M. and end not later than 6 P.M. (in workshops 9 P.M.), or else begin not before 7 A.M. and end not later than 7 P.M. On Saturdays work must end at or before 2 P.M. in textile and 4 P.M. in other factories and workshops. The meal-times shall amount to not less than two hours in the day in textile factories, and one hour and a half in other places of work, except on Saturday, when half an hour only may be allowed. The general result seems to be a working week of 56½ hours in textile factories, and 60 hours in non-textile factories and workshops, subject to exceptions, holidays, etc.

The regulations for the employment of children are of a far more complex character. The 20th section, indeed, is simple enough, absolutely prohibiting the employment in any factory or workshop of children under the age of ten years—a rule extended to industry generally by the 5th section of the Elementary Education Act of 1876, 39 and 40 Vict. cap. 79. Under sixteen years of age a certificate of fitness for factory labour must be obtained. Children are only to be worked upon the half-time system, which admits, however, two methods, either of working part of the day in the factory and another part in school, or else attending the factory and school on alternate days. On the latter system the child is treated much on the terms of a young person, but must never be employed at work for two days in succession, nor without alteration of the days in each alternate week.

In the daily half-time system, morning sets of children begin with the young persons, but end at one o'clock, and afternoon sets begin at one o'clock and end with the young persons. The morning set of one week becomes an afternoon set the next week, and *vice versâ*. The Saturday half-holiday is provided for in an elaborate way. When employed in a morning or afternoon set, a child is required to attend a recognised efficient school for one attendance every day excepting Saturday. On the alternate day system two attendances shall be made on each work day preceding each day of employment. Sunday labour is prohibited on the part of all children, young persons, and women, excepting Jews, for whom special regulations are provided. There are, moreover, all kinds of special exceptions and relaxations in particular trades. Manual labour carried on by a family in their own dwelling is exempted from restriction under section 98, provided that the labour is exercised at irregular intervals, and does not furnish the whole or principal means of living. The work of straw-plaiting, pillow-lace-making, and glove-making is expressly exempted under section 97 when carried on in a private house, and such exemption may be extended by the Secretary of State to other light, healthy handicrafts. As the terms employed do not include male persons above the age of eighteen years, except in the sections relating to safety and sanitary precautions, it follows that men are allowed to work as they like, day or night.

There are various further exceptions; thus overtime is freely allowed up to nine or ten o'clock at night, when fruit has to be suddenly preserved, or railway guides bound at the end of the month, or Christmas presents rapidly pushed forward, or some similar press of work undertaken. When water-mills are liable to be stopped by drought or flood, a certain amount of overtime may be granted by the Secretary of State to make up the loss.

A number of additional relaxations or changes have been made by order of the Secretary of State, under powers given in several sections; thus another day has been allowed to be substituted for the Saturday half-holiday in the case of printing-offices engaged in printing newspapers, railway time-tables, and other urgent publications, as also in certain workshops where clothes are being made. Other orders grant a five hours' spell in the hosiery and woollen factories of certain counties; vary the holidays; alter the meal hours; allow employment during meal hours; allow thirty minutes' overtime in case of non-completion of work, and so forth.

Adult Male Labour.—It is quite possible that, at some future time, attempts will be made to press upon the attention of the Legislature measures for the restriction of adult male labour. At present, under the Factory and Workshop Act, regulation of the time of labour is carefully limited, as already explained, to the labour of children, young persons, and women. The Legislature has, in fact, always abstained from interfering with the liberty of adult men to work as long or as short a time as they like. Indirectly, however, a large number of workmen fall practically under restriction, because, where many children or women are employed, the whole labour of the factory is brought to a stand when the clock strikes the hour assigned for stopping in the Act. It is well known, however, that many men advocate the interference of the Legislature in all factories whatsoever. The ultimatum of the working classes is expressed in the following couplet:—

> "Eight hours to work, eight hours to play;
> Eight hours to sleep, and eight shillings a day."

In the United States an Eight Hours Act has already been passed in some of the States, but being purely permissive in character, has proved to be a dead letter. An Act which defines a day's labour as being that of eight hours, in the absence of any stipulation to the contrary, is, of course, easily set aside, and has been generally disregarded.

I venture to maintain that the question of limiting adult male labour in associated and organised bodies of men is not to be decided once for all on some supposed principle of liberty. The same principle, if it existed, would apply to adult women. We must treat the question on the varied and detailed grounds of expediency. No one, indeed, would propose to interfere with the workman labouring in his own private shop or dwelling. There each man can work as he likes. But where a large number of men are employed together in a factory there is not the same individual liberty; all must conform to the wishes of the majority, or the will of the employers, or the customs of the trade. I see nothing, therefore, to forbid the State interfering in the matter, if it could be clearly shown that the existing customs are injurious to health, and that there is no other probable remedy. Neither principle, experience, nor precedent, in other cases of legislation, prevents us from contemplating the idea of State interference in such circumstances.

But we are bound in a question of this sort to place ourselves at every point of view, and to accept all kinds of information, irrespective of any strict laws of evidence. Thus, when we hear workmen debating on the moral and sanitary advantages of an Eight Hours Bill, we must remember the prevalent fallacy that the limitation of labour raises its price, and transfers some of the master's profits to the workman's pockets. To lessen the day's labour by one hour, is to lessen the supply of labour by one-ninth or one-tenth part, and to the same extent to waste the efficiency of all machinery, and of the fixed capital connected therewith. It is an economic fallacy to suppose that any adequate counterbalancing advantage can, as a general rule, arise out of this loss, except of course the recreative, sanitary, or intellectual advantages (if any) to the workman from his enjoyment of more leisure time. When we observe, too, that trades unions are already constantly wrangling with employers for a reduction of hours, while individual workmen are generally ready to work overtime for a moderate inducement, we shall be led to think that there is no ground whatever for legal limitation of adult male labour in the present day. Where the interference of trade societies is already, if anything too great, there would be harm rather than good in adding Government restrictions.

Grandmotherly Legislation.—In spite of the conclusion just arrived at, I think it well to show by example that the Legislature has fully conceded, even for adult men, the principle of "grandmotherly legislation," if principles must be spoken of. I may mention again the Truck Acts as a standing proof that men have been held to need the protection of the State in some of the simplest transactions of life. The freedom of contract is actually destroyed by such laws. It is only necessary again to mention the Coal Mines Act and the Metalliferous Mines Act (35 and 36 Vict. caps. 76, 77), or the complicated series of Acts relating to merchant shipping, to show what a mass of legislation has already been sanctioned for the protection mainly of adult men. The provisions of the law to repress crimping and imposition by the keepers of seamen's lodgings (17 and 18 Vict. cap. 104, sections 233-238) are especially a case in point. Any person can be fined five pounds who, on board a ship within twenty-four hours of her arrival, solicits a seaman to become a lodger. The seaman is treated by the law as if he were a mere child; but there is no like law to protect the bewildered traveller, who, in stepping out of the railway-station at some strange town, finds himself beset by a score of hotel porters and touts of various descriptions.

The point of the matter, however, is most curiously illustrated by the history of the law relating to the fencing of machinery. By the 7 and 8 Vict. cap. 15, sec. 21, it was enacted that "every fly-wheel . . . and every hoist or teagle, near to which children or young persons are liable to pass or be employed, and all parts of the mill-gearing in a factory, shall be securely fenced." When these words came to be critically read by those machinery owners, to whom they were a matter of pecuniary importance, it was argued that the limitation "near to which children or young persons are liable to pass" must have been intended to apply to all parts of the mill-gearing in a factory as well as to the fly-wheel, hoist, teagle, etc. The contrary supposition not only produced some absurd distinctions between parts which were always to be fenced and those which were only sometimes to be fenced, but it led to the very sweeping result that a vast amount of machinery to which men alone had access was to be fenced just as if women and children were in question. The principle of adult male protective legislation was in fact involved unintentionally in the awkward wording of the clause. The disputes which arose in consequence induced the Government to pass a special Act (the Factory Act of 1856, 19 and 20 Vict. cap. 38), for the purpose of explaining and limiting the words above quoted. It was enacted that "the said section 21, so far as the same refers to mill-gearing, shall apply only to those parts thereof with which children and young persons and women are liable to come in contact, either in passing or in their ordinary occupation in the factory." Adult males, then, were to be left to be crushed to death by their own carelessness, when so small an expenditure would render these accidents nearly impossible. Twenty years later the absurdity as well as the inhumanity of this limitation seems to have become apparent, and in the Factory and Workshop Act of 1878 the sections (5 and 6) relating to the fencing of machinery apply to "any person," which of course includes the adult male. Nor, while these sections were debated in committee, was any objection made nor any reference to the old disputes. The regulations in the same Act relating to bakehouses involve men as well as boys, but it was explained by Mr. Cross that they were intended for the good of the bread, not the good of the men. But the principle of legislation for men was sufficiently conceded in the matter of fencing.

Adult Women's Labour.—After the remarks just made upon the expediency of restrictions on adult men's labour, it may be superfluous to consider whether like restrictions are justifiable in the case of adult women. It seems to be conceded that women are less able to take care of themselves than men, and accordingly since 1833 they have been an object of care to the Legislature. No doubt, with trifling exceptions, they have formed no trades unions, and apparently have taken no measures to protect themselves. In the case of domestic service, nevertheless, they have known perfectly well how to advance their interests. It is, indeed, a remarkable fact worthy of careful notice, that while factory labour has engrossed so large a share of the attention of Parliament, and added a multitude of Acts to the Statute-Book, there is really no statute law worth speaking of which relates to domestic service. The common law, which in this case means little more than custom, has been found sufficient to secure the rights and interests of adult women as well as men. This, however, seems to indicate by contrast the need for legislation where the conditions of labour are very different. The most absolute of labour prohibitions, for instance, is that of the Act of 1842 (5 and 6 Vict. cap. 99), which declared it to be "unfit that women and girls should be employed in any mine or colliery." Everybody has acquiesced in this law, and though the circumstances of mines may be described as exceptional, so in fact in some degree are all the circumstances in which restrictive legislation has been applied. A factory where people work together in large numbers, and under necessity to remain the whole interval of time determined by the employers or by custom, is an exception to the conditions of agricultural or domestic labour which had prevailed from primeval times down to a century or two ago.

Professor Fawcett has upon every suitable occasion —especially in his powerful speech in the House of Commons on 30th July 1873—protested against interference with adult women's labour on the ground that there was no more justification for interfering with their labour than there was for interfering with the labour of men.[1] This opinion he repeated in the debates upon the Factory Act of 1878. His argument does not readily admit of answer except upon the grounds adopted generally in this essay. If the liberty of the subject, or any abstract indefeasible right, is to be recognised, Professor Fawcett cannot be answered. But if we say that legislation is a matter of circumstance, and must be guided by experience, then there are ample grounds, not only for the Mines Act of 1842, but generally for the course of legislation in regard to women. In the next section, indeed, I venture to advocate a decided advance in restrictive legislation as regards women.

Employment of Mothers.—Another question relating to the factory laws is that of the expediency of allowing the employment, as is usually said, of married, or more strictly speaking, of child-bearing women in factories and workshops. The great evil which arises from such employment is the separation of the mother from her young children. In the case of infants who ought to be suckled, the result is usually disastrous. Committed during the whole day to the care of inexperienced and uninterested nurses, they are fed on "pap"—that is, bread and water—or some mixed food hardly more suitable to an infant's stomach. A large proportion succumb, and those who, by any fortunate accident of more vigorous constitution or slightly better treatment, survive, are too often ruined physically and mentally, and grow up into a stunted and sickly generation. Im-

[1] Fawcett's "Speeches on some Current Political Questions," p. 133.

provident marriages, too, are much promoted by the fact that the mother can earn her own living. The evils arising out of the admission of mothers to the mills are in fact so palpable, and so generally admitted in the manufacturing districts, that the only question is, Are such evils remediable?

It has long, indeed, been one of the most frequent and urgent proposals of trade unionists that married women should be "taken out of the mills." The so-called labour advocates are often a great deal nearer to the truth than the general public believe. But then, unfortunately, they give reasons for their opinions, and these reasons will not always bear examination. Thus, in favour of the summary exclusion of married women, it is argued that the market is overstocked, and that if married women were taken out the operatives would realise a great social and domestic benefit, whilst "much of the overplus labour would be reduced." This, however, is obviously bad political economy. We cannot possibly increase the welfare of the people by lessening labour, the source of wealth. But there is another possible aspect of the matter. It must not be necessarily assumed that the amount of earnings is the measure of advantages enjoyed. Those who know not how to spend well are often injured rather than bettered by higher earnings; and when these earnings are acquired at the cost of neglecting a young family and destroying the home, the evils may become such as to demand the attention of the Legislature. The doctrine of the liberty of the subject will of course crop up again. On what ground, it will be asked, can we presume to think of preventing an adult woman, not uncommonly an unmarried woman, with full legal rights, from working where she pleases? In this case the answer is particularly easy and conclusive. On the ground that the first duty of a mother is to give that sustenance to her infant which she alone can give in perfection. Now the Factory Act practically obliges a woman who works under it to remain at work four and a half hours at a spell, which is about twice the interval which should elapse between the meals of a very young infant. The result is that suckling is abandoned, or, what is perhaps still worse, an alternation of artificial and of deteriorated natural food is given to the child. In any case the interests of a future generation are sacrificed to the apparent good of the present, and the foundation is laid for multitudinous evils in the future. Hence arises a considerable part of the shocking infantile mortality prevailing in many parts of the manufacturing districts, accompanied by much immorality and intemperance not unnaturally produced by the destruction of home influences.

As some incredulity seems to exist in England as to the expediency and practicability of legislation concerning this subject, it may be well to mention that the Social Science Association of Germany, according to Mr. Mundella, warmly advocates the entire exclusion of married women from factory labour. The subject has also been carefully investigated by Mr. Carroll D. Wright, the chief, and Mr. George H. Long, the deputy-chief, of the Massachusetts Statistical Bureau. Their conclusions, as stated in the Sixth Annnal Report of the Bureau, published in March 1875 (Public Document, No. 31), are in such striking accord with the views here advocated that I must make some brief quotations. On pp. 183-4 the American statisticians denounce the employment of married women (*i.e.* mothers), as "at once the most harmful wrong, and the most difficult to reach." With some deprecation of popular opinion they pronounce "that married women ought not to be tolerated in mills at all. Vital science will one day demand their exclusion; but *we* certainly can recommend the regulation of their work." As to the effect of such employment upon the health and welfare of the offspring, they conclude—"it is an evil that is sapping the life of our operative population, and must sooner or later be regulated, or, more probably, stopped."

In the paragraph which I quote below, the American statisticians explain what has not received proper attention here, namely, that the employment of a married woman under the Acts practically defeats the intention of those Acts, inasmuch as she has domestic work to perform in addition to a full day's work at the mills. They say—

"We find it a difficult subject to treat, so many obstacles come up, so many seemingly insurmountable barriers, so much that smacks of sentimentalism, but still speaks to one's highest appreciation of real justice and mercy, and to one's sympathy for the helpless who now must be raised in such a way as to entail constant expense, when, by proper treatment and deprivation from immediate earnings, comfort and strength for old age would be secured. It is a knotty point, and one which must demand the attention of philanthropists and law-makers, as it already has of mill-owners, and which will soon call for serious consideration; but it is so delicate and so knotty, we can at the present time do little more than enter an earnest appeal for this class of workers, which has, as a class by itself, been overlooked in the desire to establish some more noisy reforms. To be sure, married women have received, or will receive, what benefits accrue from the ten-hour law; but when it is considered that no ten-hour law can ever be put into practical operation by the mother of a family, even when she has nothing but her family to attend to, it will be readily seen how utterly impossible it is for such law to reach the woman who does ten hours' work in the mill, cooks for her husband and children, and cares for the household. It is a slavery which must be abolished or alleviated; and, if we succeed in drawing the attention of earnest practical men to the subject, we shall have no fear but the intelligence of the citizens of Massachusetts will, at an early day, remove the evil."

So great are the social evils thus arising that no doubt can exist as to the propriety of legislative interference could a practicable method be devised which would not entail counterbalancing evils. There are as usual many possible courses. Summary and immediate exclusion of mothers from factory work is out of the question, so considerable are the numbers concerned, and so difficult the position into which many women have brought themselves by thoughtless marriages. Some intermediate and palliative measure is therefore requisite, such as the permission of employment for mothers at those factories only where well-supervised *crèches* are provided by the employers, the mother being permitted to break the morning and afternoon spells in order to suckle her child. This system has been carried into effect in some French factories with much success; and it is regularly adopted in many laundries. Even without legislative interference much good would be done if employers would make it a rule to inquire into the circumstances of married or child-bearing women, and only to give employment where there are no young children to be injured, or where, on consideration of all the circumstances, more harm than good would be done by refusal. This system has long been maintained by a large firm of cotton thread manufacturers in Glasgow. It would be even more advantageous in the case of any large isolated factory which furnishes the sole employment of the neighbourhood. I will not, however, further dwell upon this subject here, because I have recently treated it at some length in the *Contemporary Review* for January 1882 (vol. xli. pp. 37-53), where will be found a good deal of evidence concerning the evils in question, and some suggestions as to the best form of remedy.

Apprenticeship or Industrial Slavery of Youths.—A subject well worthy of attention, but which receives little, is that of apprenticeship, and the terms under which young persons are educated to a trade. An admirable article, to be found both in the *Penny* and the *English Cyclopædias*, and in Knight's *Political Dictionary*, gives a detailed history of the law and practice of apprenticeship. The binding of young persons to serve masters was unknown to the Romans and the Roman law. Its origin is to be sought in the mediæval guilds from the twelfth century onwards, the purpose being obviously to combine instruction with that limitation of numbers entering a trade, which was always a prime point of guild policy. Subsequently to the twelfth century apprenticeship prevailed in all the more advanced nations of Europe—in France, Germany, Italy, and Spain, as well as England. According to Adam Smith, seven years was the usual term of the engagement in all trades and countries. But it is probable that there was no settled rule. The number seven probably prevailed from the superstitions or traditional reasons which made it predominate in many human institutions. Apprenticeship is first incidentally noticed in the English Statute-Book in the year 1388 (12 Rich. II. cap. 3). From the 7 Henry IV. cap. 17 (1405-6) we learn that apprenticeship had become a common practice—so common that this law was intended to prevent children from going into trades and to retain them as agricultural labourers. In another Act (8 Henry VI. cap. 11) the taking of apprentices is stated to have been at that time a custom of London time out of mind. The whole law of the subject was consolidated and perfected by the celebrated Statute of Apprentices (5 Eliz. cap. 4) of which the second half, sections 25 to 48, is almost exclusively occupied in defining the term of apprenticeship in various trades. The general rule was (sec. 36) that no one could be apprenticed other than such as be under the age of twenty-one years, which section, together with the prohibitions in section 31, was intended to prevent any person from entering a handicraft unless he were brought up to it when young. The term of apprenticeship was to be seven years at least (sec. 26), "so as the term and years of such apprentice do not expire or determine afore such apprentice shall be of the age of twenty-four years at the least." Apparently, then, every apprentice to a manual occupation was bound to remain in such position up to the age of twenty-four years at least, though it is provided (sec. 25) that in agriculture twenty-one years may be the end of the term.

We must suppose that the clauses of this great but noxious Act relating to apprentices were found more practicable and less tyrannical than those relating to adult workmen, for they long remained in operation in the trades which existed at the epoch of the Act. As elsewhere remarked, newly invented occupations were exempt under section 31 from the restrictions of the statute, so that apprenticeship was in them optional. A seven years' apprenticeship was, however, for a long time the customary mode of entering all trades, and the custom survives even to the present day. It is a curious fact, too, that even in those trades, such as the woollen manufacture, which were legally under the Statute of Apprentices, the law of Elizabeth was entirely forgotten, being known neither to masters nor men. The custom of the seven years' apprenticeship was, however, traditionally established, and a long struggle arose when manufacturers began in the newly-built mills to introduce women and children who had served no apprenticeship. Combinations of woollen weavers were at length formed to endeavour to maintain the custom, and they seem in time to have discovered the existence of the Elizabethan law. While Parliament, on the one hand, was occupied in endeavouring to suppress combinations of workmen, these workmen succeeded in prosecuting several employers and convicting them for breaches of the Statute of Apprentices. As, however, the enforcement of the law would have thrown great numbers of working people out of employment, Parliament resorted in 1803 to the device of suspending the laws of apprenticeship,—a suspension renewed in successive years until they were repealed in 1809 (49 Geo. III. cap. 109).

Thus at length died apprenticeship as the statutory mode of entering trades. The recent entire repeal of the 5 Eliz. cap. 4, and of various other statutes relating to the subject, has left little written law on the subject except what relates to parish or marine apprentices. But there undoubtedly still remains the common-law power on the part of parents of binding their children apprentices, and so recent a law as the Employers and Workmen Act (1875) recognises the custom by providing for the settlement of disputes between master and apprentices (sections 5 to 7). Such disputes are to be determined by courts of summary jurisdiction as if they were between employers and workmen. The justices may indeed rescind the instrument of apprenticeship, ordering the whole or any part of the premium to be repaid. But they may also order the apprentice to perform his duties, and if he fails they may, after the expiration of one month, imprison him for a period not exceeding fourteen days. This, moreover, may be done "from time to time," which is understood to mean that after one order of performance the justices may impose any succession of fourteen-day terms of imprisonment upon a refractory apprentice. Except, then, by the consent of the parties, or the merciful discretion of the justices in rescinding the indentures, the apprentice is in the position of a slave to his master, bound to fulfil his reasonable orders under the constant penalty of imprisonment.

There is reason to hope and believe, indeed, that the practice of binding youths to long terms of apprenticeship is falling into desuetude. The demand for boys' labour in factories, shops, workshops, the telegraph service, etc., is so great that the youths are masters of the situation; they can choose their employment, and ask fair wages as well. Thus in many trades journeymen are glad to get intelligent youths as assistants, without insisting on a long term of service. As the intelligence of children is raised under the Education and Factory Acts this tendency will still further develop itself. In fact, the seven years' indentures can only be required in some few trades which by combination succeed in limiting their numbers. The question may well admit of discussion, therefore, whether on every ground the common law, allowing a parent to bind his child to a long term of industrial servitude, ought not to be abolished almost entirely. The law and practice is such as to give the master a vastly greater power than the parent himself. The child is bound at an age when he can have no sure judgment nor choice of a trade, and once bound there is no further choice. There is no field for the display of inclination or talent. Surely the power of the parent thus to divest himself of his responsibilities is altogether anomalous, and in operation often little short of barbarous. It is now simply a *survival*, an obsolete relic of a former state of things. There is, however, little need to argue about the matter, because the greatest authorities have denounced the custom. Adam Smith (*Wealth of Nations*, Book I. chap. x. part ii.) especially has condemned long apprenticeships in well-known passages.

"The institution of long apprenticeships has no tendency to form young people to industry. A journeyman who works by the piece is likely to be industrious, because he derives a benefit from every exertion of his industry. An apprentice is likely to be idle, and almost always is so, because he has no immediate interest to be otherwise. . . . A young man naturally conceives an aversion to labour, when for a long time he receives no benefit from it. . . . A young man would practise with much more diligence and attention, if from the beginning he wrought as a journeyman, being paid in proportion to the little work which he could execute, and paying in his turn for the materials which he might sometimes spoil through awkwardness and inexperience. His education would generally in this way be more effectual, and always less tedious and expensive."

These opinions of Smith have been to a great extent borne out by the disuse of apprenticeship in many trades. What remains of the practice is a survival which ought to be put an end to. Inquiry would, no doubt, be needed as to the exact mode of doing this. Probably a father ought not to be allowed to hire out his child for a longer term than one year at a time; in any case, apprenticeships should be limited to three years. Such a tyrannical power as that possessed by the justices of forcing a young person to work at an unwelcome trade under the fear of constantly-renewed imprisonment should be repealed, as befitting the Middle Ages rather than the reign of Victoria.

Since the above remarks were first drafted, the public has been startled by the case of the unfortunate youths brought home from Constantinople by Mr. Littler, Q.C. It was actually suggested in the Police Court that the law against slavery would apply in the case of these youths;

but the magistrate held that apprenticeship bonds duly executed held good against that law. The Englishman is engaged in putting down slavery in all parts of the world, but is unaware that parents can and do sell their own children into slavery and wretchedness here in London itself, under the forms of a law which ought to be regarded as a mere survival from semi-barbarous times. And although a child is legally an infant, and incapable of most legal acts below the age of twenty-one years, yet his nominal consent, even at a very tender age, is held sufficient to consign him to industrial slavery up to the age of legal majority!

Shop Assistants' Labour.—An important but hitherto little regarded kind of industry is that of men, women, and young persons employed in retail shops and warehouses. Where the work done is simply that of trade, as distinguished from manufacture, the State has hitherto held entirely aloof. The distinction is clearly an artificial one in many cases; the making up of pounds of sugar and the packing of goods is clearly a manual operation, or sometimes a machine operation, identical with much that is done in factories. Grocers' assistants, too, are frequently employed in grinding coffee, chopping loaf sugar, mixing teas, and the like. As a shopman or woman seldom sits down during the hours of work, the labour is exhausting in the long-run. In the character of the work itself there is no reason why it should not be regulated as much as various handicrafts. The anomaly of the distinction drawn by the law is strongly marked in the case of some establishments where persons employed upstairs under the Factory and Workshop

Act are brought downstairs to assist in the shop as soon as the legal hour has struck upon the clock.

We must assume, then, that the hours of shop assistants' labour remain unregulated from regard to the convenience of the public, or else from regard to the profits of the employers. But the interests of the employers have not been allowed to stand in the way of the creation of the Factory Acts. It seems, then, that it is the public necessity or convenience which keeps shops open to ten or twelve o'clock at night, and obliges shop assistants to labour, in many cases, from fourteen to eighteen, or even nineteen hours in the twenty-four.

It is well known that neither the shop people nor the philanthropic public acquiesce entirely in this state of things. The existence of many early closing associations shows the prevailing discontent. Considerable success has been achieved in some towns or parts of towns by these associations, and most high-class shops now close at six or seven o'clock, or nearly as early as we should think desirable. But in the east end of London and other poor localities the hours of closing are still very late, especially on Saturday night. The difficulty of the matter is clearly that of competition. Jones has a well-grounded fear that if he closes his shop at 7 P.M., his rival Brown will enjoy all the better trade until 9 or 10. Such gain of customers may eventually enable Brown to drive Jones out of the trade altogether. Failure in the competition of retail trade may mean ruin. No ordinary tradesman, then, can singly break through the custom of the locality. It is obvious, too, that as a chain may break from the defect of a single link, so the defection of a single grocer from an early closing association may oblige all the other grocers to withdraw. Only a strong spirit of trades unionism, or else the abstention of the public, or, in the last resort, legislative interference, can effect early closing.

I venture to think that the early closing of shops in so-called respectable neighbourhoods is mainly due to the fact that richer customers usually go home to dinner between 6 and 7 P.M., and, owing to our *laisser faire* system of moral legislation, ladies especially are obliged to retire from the streets about that time. The working-classes, on the contrary, having come from their employment at some time between half-past five and seven o'clock, are then prepared, if not obliged, to begin their shopping. If this be the state of the case, it seems to be very doubtful whether any considerable change will be effected without the intervention of the Legislature. As there can be no doubt about the advantage of shorter hours to the shop people, the only remaining questions regard the convenience of the public, and the practicability of enforcing a restrictive law. As to the latter point, Mr. Henderson, one of the inspectors of factories in the Metropolis, expressed considerable doubt, in his evidence before the Factory Acts Commission. Considering, however, that shops depend for their trade upon publicity, and that competitors in trade would have the strongest possible motives for exposing each other's infractions of the law, I cannot see the practical difficulties. An inspector, by merely walking down a street of shops after the legal hour of closing, would discover the infractions without much difficulty.

The real point to consider, therefore, is whether the

public, especially the working-class public, would suffer. Judging from their present habits of shopping up to ten o'clock at night, and twelve o'clock on Saturday nights, they would suffer. It can hardly, indeed, be supposed that anybody is driven by necessity to buy clothes, furniture, and other permanent articles, after eight o'clock. The case may be somewhat different with food, tobacco, drinks, and other matters of immediate need. Some doubt may arise as to whether the brightly-lighted streets of a poor neighbourhood do not really form the promenade ground of those who have few pleasures to relieve the dull monotonous round of a laborious life. To those who live in crowded dirty lodgings unsavoury streets may be a breathing-place, and the well-filled shop windows the only available museum of science and art. Much care and discrimination would obviously be needed, and a legislator might find the question almost as thorny as that of public-house closing and the *bonâ fide* traveller. In any case, it is necessary to approach the question tentatively and gradually. The experiment might, moreover, be tried at first in such separate towns as should present strong petitions in favour of it; but to prevent unfair competition the law should apply to the whole of a town, if to any part. The regulation might even be carried out by special clauses in local Acts of Parliament, in the same way that the municipal authorities of Manchester and Liverpool are endeavouring to remedy the great abuse of young children trading in the streets at night. Such special legislation no doubt needs to be watched, but when properly watched presents the best method of gaining experience. It amounts, in fact, to experimental legislation.

Agricultural Labour.—Very little can be said in this book on the subject of agricultural labourers. The "hind," as he now exists in the rural parts of England, is mainly the result of the Land Laws and the Poor Laws, subjects of great extent and importance which have little affinity with the special topic of this essay, and are treated in other volumes of the same series. In former centuries the agricultural labourer, in common with all other labourers, came within the scope of the Statute of Labourers, the Statute of Apprentices, and other similar laws; but since such kind of legislation became obsolete, the real peasant, so far as he has been allowed to exist at all, has not been vexed with much legislation. Even the Truck Act, as we have seen, does not apply to him. A family living on their ancestral farm, and cultivating it with their united labour, represent so natural and healthy a condition of life that little or no interference of the State is needed. But bad laws, especially bad Poor Laws, not to speak of bad Game Laws, have in England caused the peasant to diverge sadly from this state of things. The laws of pauper settlement led to the general destruction of labourers' cottages wherever they could possibly be destroyed. The labourers were obliged to crowd together in the nearest village or town. Hence, whenever much labour was needed for the cultivation of root and other special crops, gangs of men, boys, women, and children had to be employed, in a manner giving rise to scandalous results. As it was impossible all at once to reverse the course of events which led to these abuses, the only resource was to regulate agricultural gangs, a work attempted in the 30 and 31 Vict. cap. 130. This Act provided that every person acting as gang-master should previously obtain a license from the justices, on proof that he was a person of good character, and fit to be trusted with the control of a gang. No child under eight years of age was to be employed; no females were to work in the same gang as men; and, when females were employed, a licensed female gang-mistress was to be present. From the first the Act was to a great extent evaded or disregarded. Although penalties were imposed upon every breach of the Act, no machinery of inspection or prosecution was provided; it was nobody's business to see that the Act was observed, and it was therefore not observed.

Shortly after the passing of this Act were published the elaborate inquiries of the Commission appointed in 1867 to investigate the employment of children, young persons, and women in agriculture.[1] The facts brought to light showed abundant scope for State interference, but no useful results have followed except as regards the compulsory education of agricultural children. This was specially provided for by the Agricultural Children Act, 1873 (36 and 37 Vict. cap. 67), which, however, was repealed for no very clear reason by the Elementary Education Act of 1876, the provisions of which were substituted. But section 16 of the Agricultural Children Act had already repealed so much of the fourth section of the Agricultural Gangs Act as related to children, and this repeal holds good. It seems to follow that the remainder of this fourth section, relating to mixed gangs and female gang-mistresses, probably entirely inoperative, together with the provisions of the Elementary Educa-

[1] Parliamentary Papers, 1867-8 [4068 and i.], 1868-9 [4202 and i.]

tion Acts, forms practically the sum total of direct restrictive legislation now applying to agriculture. Here is a wonderful contrast to the elaborate regulations of the factory, workshop, shipping, coal mines, metalliferous mines, and other Acts relating to the various branches of manufacturing and commercial industry. It would lead us too far to inquire whether this absence of legislative restriction is due to its needlessness, or to the unwillingness of landowning legislators to touch the interests of their own order.

CHAPTER IV

INDIRECT INTERFERENCE WITH INDUSTRY—TRADES UNION LEGISLATION

HAVING now considered the application of the principles of industrial legislation as manifested in the direct interference of the State, we have yet the larger and more difficult part of the subject before us. Individuals are in the habit of interfering with their neighbours' affairs, and in the case of trade and industry such interference has from early times assumed a decided form. Common trade interest is one of the strongest and most frequent bonds of society, and, judged by the light of history, is likely always to be a considerable factor in social affairs. It leads to the creation of secret or open confederacies attempting to control not only their own members, but all whose actions touch the trade interest. *Imperia in imperio* are continually growing up, and, under the guise or name of guilds, fraternities, colleges, corporations, friendly societies, trades unions, institutes or associations of various titles assume a right of government. It thus becomes a highly important and difficult question for the State to decide how such bodies can be treated. The State in controlling the individual must, of course, control his control over other individuals, where that becomes noxious to the community. This task, however, is one of great difficulty, owing to the secret and insidious forms which trade confederacy assumes when prohibited, and the insensible way in which it varies in degree from perfectly legitimate discussion to distinct conspiracy, enforced occasionally by criminal outrage.

History of Trade Societies.—It is always needful to view the present by the light of the past, but more especially so in the case of trade societies. We learn from history that such societies are among the earliest and most persistent institutions of the human race. In the Old Testament, for instance, are to be found allusions to a guild of apothecaries (Nehemiah iii. 8, and other passages, as specified in Mr. Spencer's *Descriptive Sociology*, No. 7, p. 103). In the Roman State trade societies arose at least as early as the time of Publius Servilius, under whose reign existed a *collegium mercatorum.* The Roman law, however, was very jealous of the existence of any such bodies, and in the Digest we find that the formation of collegia was prohibited unless under the authority of the Emperor or a Senatus-Consultum (Digest 47, tit. 22, ss. 1, 2, 3). No doubt in Roman Britain such collegia opificum existed; nevertheless the first origin of modern trade societies must be traced to the guilds of the rude Teutonic tribes. Space totally fails me here to allow description of the three kinds of guilds—Frith or Peace guilds, religious guilds, and trade guilds—which undoubtedly existed in Saxon times, the charters of some of them being extant in Thorpe's *Diplomatarium Anglicum.* The laws of Ina, Alfred, and Athelstan mention and recognise such bodies, and even if some societies such as the Freemasons have not a continuous history from the line of Athelstan to the present day, certain it is that trade guilds have never been wanting; the City Companies still meeting in their guild halls are the lineal descendants in a degenerated form of the Saxon guilds. For the whole history of the mediæval guilds I must refer the reader to the essay of Brentano "On the History and Development of Guilds, and the Origin of Trades Unions," prefixed to the invaluable collection of documents given in Toulmin Smith's English Guilds (Early English Text Society), also issued separately. Brentano's own views on industrial legislation should be read *cum grano*, but his history is excellent. A great amount of information is also given in Mr. C. Walford's *Insurance Cyclopædia*, vol. v. article "Guilds."

As the relations of labour and capital turn mainly upon economic considerations, and as the theory of the subject has been much misunderstood and perverted even by economists, I commence with the briefest possible exposition of what I conceive to be the true theory of the mechanics of production.

Economics of the Labour Question.—The economics of the labour question may be stated in a manner brief and simple enough. Production of wealth consists in the putting together of certain materials, and the working them up into some novel form by the aid of labour—that is, by muscular force and mental skill and knowledge. As with the Witches' Cauldron, there is needed

> "Double, double toil and trouble;
> Fire burn and cauldron bubble."

The point of the matter is that, like the contents of the cauldron, the results of production form a joint result or medley. All the constituents are thrown into hotch-potch, and as it is impossible to say what part of the product is due to any of the contributions thrown into the cauldron, no natural, necessary, or legal principle of dividing the proceeds can be assigned. If, indeed, all the elements of production, the materials as well as the labour and skill of management, are all due to one person, he of course owns the whole of the products, and no question of distribution arises. The product is neither wages, profit, interest nor rent, nor any combination of these. It is wealth or commodity simply.

Under the complex arrangements of modern industry, however, the several requisites which go to the production of commodity, such as cotton cloth, are contributed by different persons and classes of persons. One person owns the land on which the mill stands; another builds the mill and stocks it with machinery; the work-people furnish what might seem the most essential of all—the labour which actually produces the cloth. But where all are essential there can be no question of degree and precedence. The finished product is the joint product of all that was requisite to produce it. Quite clearly, too, the wealth to be earned by all those concerned is to be found in the aggregate product of the work after being sold. Rent, profit, interest, and wages must all be paid out of the proceeds of the business, which is in modern trade the money value of the produce.

But the difficult question now arises, on what principle or system, if any, the value of the joint product is to be shared among the landowners, capitalists, managers, and workmen who have contributed to its production. Property in result cannot possibly be traced, as we have seen, through the complex process of manufacture. Hence it may be safely said that there is no natural principle, certainly no single and simple principle, on which the division can be effected. No person's share being defined, each must ask for the most which he has any chance of getting, and must content himself with the best which he succeeds in securing. Every contributor enters voluntarily into the hotch-potch, and he cannot demand more than was agreed upon when he entered the partnership. Practically, the whole question resolves itself into a complex case of the laws of supply and demand. If any intended partner in the work of production is dissatisfied with his assigned share of the expected produce, he is at liberty to refuse to enter into the business. The other partners then must either concede his demands, or must find somebody else to take his place, or must abandon the work. The whole adjustment of distribution of wealth thus hinges upon the question whether one person or thing will do as well as another. A landlord cannot successfully ask a certain rent for his land if another landlord is willing to let an equally good and available site at a lower rent. A workman cannot expect to get forty shillings a week, while an equally good workman is ready to work at thirty-five shillings. As to simple money capital, it matters little whence it comes, provided it can be had for a sufficient term, and the smallest fractional difference in the rate of interest would therefore be a sufficient cause of preference. The same principle holds true, likewise, of the business capacity of the manager, though in a less obvious manner. It all comes to this, that the price which the owner of any kind of property, whether land, labour, or capital, can demand is limited by the price at which further supplies of the same kind can be found. In other words, all like articles must be sold at the same price when they come into competition with each other in the same market.

Obviously, then, the rate of wages which workmen can demand will depend upon the relation of supply to demand of such particular kind of labour. The demand depends upon the expected value of the produce. If a certain kind of commodity is much wanted by consumers, it means that considerable quantities can be sold at a fair or high price. There will therefore be money value in plenty to be divided between landowners, capitalists, and labourers. But if the production of such commodity requires a peculiar skill in certain of the workmen such as happens to be enjoyed by few men, there is no limitation by competition, and any price can be obtained by that skill and labour, provided, indeed, that the shares of the other producers are not reduced below what they could acquire in other occupations. The whole affair, therefore, is one of comparative advantages, each contributor to the hotch-potch trying to get the largest share of the proceeds, short of the point at which he will drive the other contributors to find other hotch-potches where their shares will be better. There is this further complication in the matter, that, as the proceeds of production depend both upon the quantity of commodity produced, and the price at which it can be sold to consumers, there is no limit to the earnings of a producer except the inclinations and means of the consumer—that is to say, the portion of other persons' productions which he is able and willing to give in exchange. The earnings of a labourer may therefore be large, either because he can produce much commodity, or because what he produces being much valued exchanges for a large share of other labourers' products. There thus arise two possible modes of increasing earnings: the one being to increase products, so as to have more to sell, and the second to decrease products in order to sell them at a higher price. But there is this obvious and all-important difference between these courses, that the latter tends to impoverish all persons except the producer, whereas the former tends to enrich both the producer and those whom he supplies. It follows inevitably that if many or all people pursued the latter policy it would fail altogether; it can only succeed by the few enriching themselves at the expense of the many; whereas the former policy of increasing products enriches alike the giver and the receiver. It is twice blessed, and is capable of unlimited adoption by all parties.

A False Theory of Wages.—The view above stated of the economics, or, as it might be called, the mechanics of production, is so obviously true and so entirely in accordance with facts that it might seem hardly to need the emphasis here given to it.[1] Nevertheless this view differs fundamentally from the two theories (for mere theories

[1] This view of the economics of industry appears to be nearly coincident with that put forth by the eminent American economist, Professor Francis A. Walker, in his standard work on "The Wages Question: a Treatise on Wages and the Wages Class;" London,

they are) of the relations of capital and labour now or recently prevailing. The first of these theories is known as the wage-fund theory of the books on political economy. It represents the rate of wages as depending upon the amount of capital which employers think proper to disburse as wages. The wages rate was regarded as the dividend, found by dividing the wages fund by the number of labourers. But, though this division doubtless takes place, there is nothing in the theory to determine either the whole amount which is to be divided, or the proportional share which any particular labourer may obtain. Nobody can possibly suppose that workmen in different branches of production, or in different ranks of the same branch, receive the same wages.

Nor can anybody imagine that the capitalist distributes his capital simply because it is his capital, irrespective of the produce which he expects from the labour bought. The relations between the producer and consumer are complicated and obscured by the fact that the real producer seldom comes into relation with the real consumer, whom he serves. The process of production takes a long time to complete, and middlemen intervene, who buy up the produce of one in order to sell again to another. In his capacity of capitalist, the owner and manager of a mill buys up the share of the eventual proceeds which the factory hand may expect to receive. The labourer cannot or will not wait many weeks; he wants to spend the value of his labour.

1878 (Macmillan); but the same view may be traced in the writings of Mr. Longe, the late Professor Cliffe Leslie, and others. This is not the place to inquire into the niceties of the history of economic doctrine.

Hence his wages are paid, and spent, and consumed, weeks, or months, or even years, before the useful effect of his labour is enjoyed by consumers. The capitalist bridges over this period and discounts the labourer's share.

But it is not the less true that, in the long-run, the wages are a share, not of the capitalist's property, but of the products which that capital assists the labourer to produce. Obviously, the amount which the capitalist will advance to any particular workman is not the amount which he possibly has to advance, but the value of the product which he expects to receive, taken in connection with what would be sufficient to pay for equally good labour by other men. Cases, of course, constantly occur where the labourer is quite ignorant and indifferent as to what is to be the result of his labour; he simply does what he is asked, and gets his customary pay. But even this ignorance will not necessarily deprive him or his class from receiving in the long-run their due share. For if some highly profitable means of employing such labour arises, many capitalists will engage in the work, and, in the absence of abundant supplies of such labour, will be obliged to attract fresh supplies by raising the rate of wages. But it is evidently the produce in prospect and not the mere possession of capital which induces this demand for labour.

Another False Theory.—The view here adopted of the economics of industry differs also from that of many members of trades unions, who appear to think that their wages actually come out of their employers' pockets. Inasmuch as the employer palpably hands over the wages, it would seem that the more they receive the less he can retain. There is no more fallacy in this idea than in the theory of a good many economists who have held that as wages rise profits must fall. But any such theory is not only obviously defective in itself, but is opposed to facts. It overlooks the fact that the amount received by the employer is unfixed, depending, as we have seen, both on the amount of goods produced and on the price at which the goods can be sold. Even assuming that the former factor cannot be raised, it may be open to the producer to raise the price of his goods, and thus recoup himself for increased payments of wages. Whether he can or cannot do so depends upon the state of the market, and especially upon the question whether other producers are under like circumstances. There are, of course, exceptional cases in which a heedless or unfortunate employer may really have to pay out of his own pocket the increased wages of his work-people, as when he has made long-continuing contracts, or has commenced production in the wrong part of the commercial cycle. But such mishaps are more or less foreseen and discounted by capitalists, who look to exceptional profits in brisk times to balance these exceptional losses. Employers must earn on the average the customary profits due to their capital and skill, otherwise the greater attractions of other branches of trade will draw capital away. Certainly the employer will no more pay wages out of his own private fortune than a wine merchant would pay the wine duties. All such duties are paid by one hand, but charged to another, namely the consumer, and so it is, as a general rule, with all other costs of production. The capitalist, like the merchant, is but an intermediary who gets goods ready for the consumer, and presents him in the price a complete bill of costs.

So far is it from being true that high wages imply loss on the employer's part, that the opposite result will often follow. Such high wages usually arise from circumstances occasioning scarcity and high price of products. Now, on higher-priced goods the employer will usually get a larger gross profit, even though the rate be no higher than in ordinary times. But it may, moreover, be possible for the employer to run up the price of his goods more than in proportion to the rise of wages, and he may thus net a considerable profit. Certainly the efforts made by miners to limit the output of coal and to raise wages during the coal famine of 1873-74 led to enormous gains on the part of many coal-owners.

The result which emerges is that the supposed conflict of labour with capital is a delusion. The real conflict is between producers and consumers. The capitalist employer is a part of the producing system, and his conflict is naturally with the consumer who buys from him. But his function of acting as discounter of the labourer's share gives rise to a further conflict with the labouring class. Thus it comes to pass that the capitalist is buffeted about and bears the whole brunt of the economic battle, while the consumer always smarts in the end.

Imaginary Right to a Trade.—A question which really lies at the basis of many past and present disputes about labour is whether a workman can claim any right of property in his skill. It may be at least plausibly said that in his education and training a skilled operative expends no small amount of capital, which remains invested in him, to be repaid by an annuity of higher wages during his available working life. Any change in trade which tends to supplant the skill thus acquired may seem to be an invasion of property almost as distinctly as if a landowner were turned out of his estate. Such arguments, however, can hardly be urged either from an economic or, in the present state of the law, from a legal point of view. We have nothing here to do with rights of property in land, which are peculiar in their nature, owing to the fact that land is necessarily limited and exclusive, each portion of each other portion, so that it must become sooner or later the monopolised property of some person or body of persons. But labour is the primary possession of every person; it represents the economic value of the person, and in respect of the greatest number is the sole source of sustenance.

Anything, then, which tends to interfere with the exercise by any person of the utmost amount of skill of which he is capable, is *primâ facie* opposed to the interests of the community. There may, as we have seen and shall further see, be counterbalancing advantages which, as in the case of registered medical practitioners and others, justify a certain restriction of industry in a few cases. But these partial monopolies must be fully justified and carefully regulated by the State. Their *raison d'être* must be the good of the people outside, not that of the privileged few inside the monopoly; and when they fail to secure this advantage they must be either reformed or destroyed. But it is, of course, a totally different matter for any body of labourers to endeavour to monopolise a trade without public sanction. The presumption, usually confirmed by experience, is that they intend such monopoly for their own benefit, not for that of the public. The only possible answer is that a trade society by maintaining regulations, by insisting upon adequate training or apprenticeship as the means of entry, and by raising a high *esprit de corps*, may really serve the public better than an entirely disaggregated body. Such, for instance, is the plea put forward in defence of those arrant trades unions—the Inns of Court. But the obvious retort is that if they are thus anxious to serve the public, they must allow the public to judge of the manner in which the service is to be performed.

The Original Plan of Modern Trades Unions.—Nor, as we have elsewhere seen, is the common law more favourable to monopoly, the uniform doctrine of which has been that restraint of trade is illegal, and may even be punished as a misdemeanour. The case was, no doubt, different so long as the Statute of Apprentices remained a part of the letter of the law. It might fairly be argued that, when the condition of entry into a trade was by law apprenticeship of at least seven years, persons who, to use the old expression, "intromitted" themselves into the trade without due apprenticeship, invaded legal property. This, accordingly, was the ground upon which many petitions of working-men were grounded when a parliamentary committee considered the proposed repeal of the Statute of Apprentices in 1813. Some time previously, in the very year which became an epoch by the publication of the *Wealth of Nations*, there was printed a very remarkable pamphlet, which more than any other publication known to me discloses the origin and principle of modern trades unions. I should suppose that this pamphlet is now an exceedingly rare document, as I know no copy except that in the British Museum, of which the press mark is 1029, i. 6 (6). (See Catalogue *ad verbum* "*Plan.*") It bears a long title, as follows:—

"A practicable and eligible plan to secure the rights and privileges of mechanics: with proper directions for the journeymen, whereby they may get an advancement in their wages without loss of time or hindrance of business. Humbly submitted to the perusal of the community at large by the Author. London, 1776."

This ably written tract urges the general establishment of trades unions. The journeymen of every shop in a parish were to send one deputy to a parish meeting of the trade, at which an agent for the parish was to be selected out of their number. The parish agents, again, were to meet at times to elect a special or grand committee with proper salaries. Masters were eligible equally with the journeymen, and half the special committee might consist of them. There might also be two gentlemen not of the calling. All members were to pay one shilling a month. All strangers before getting employment in the metropolis were to apply to one of the clerks of the society and get a certificate of having entered themselves as a member. Before leaving London they were to get certificates to carry into the country. The grand committee were to make use of every lawful means in their power to preserve their rights inviolate, and to prevent those from exercising the calling who were not authorised by law, whether as journeymen or masters. Those, however, were to be accepted who had followed the trade prior to the establishment of the proposed society. These arrangements, it was hoped, would "deter those from communicating the secrets of our trade, whose duty it is most to conceal them." The committee were further to avail themselves of every information, and to pursue every legal mode to prevent any person from working at "our" calling who refuses to comply with the articles and resolutions of this society.

This plan, it will be at once seen, anticipates the whole principles and mode of working of modern trades unions. Societies appear actually to have been formed on the basis sketched out, for, in Brentano's work (p. 110), we find mention of an advertisement in 1802 calling a meeting of one weaver out of the parish he represents, in order to determine on prosecuting those who unlawfully exercise or follow the trade of a weaver. But the parish area was afterwards abandoned by societies, and the limits of districts selected as might be most convenient. Masters, again, have not in recent times taken the prominent place assigned to them in the "Plan," although in many trades it has been the practice to require both foremen and employers to belong to the society at least formally. In all other respects the *raison d'être* and the principles of action of trade societies are faithfully sketched out in this remarkable pamphlet. One of the ablest passages, however, is that in which the writer in a few words puts the whole question of the right to a trade before us. He says (p. 14):—

"It has been frequently objected that to deprive an ingenious man of the liberty to exercise his abilities merely because his parents had it not in their power to put him apprentice, and permit another of meaner parts to prosecute business, only because he has enjoyed such an advantage, is notoriously unjust and glaringly partial: to which I answer, such is the imperfection of all human laws, that in their operation some individuals are always prejudiced; and the nearest approaches we can make to justice is by preferring the good of the whole to that of a part. Whenever, therefore, the exercise of an individual's abilities invades the rights of a whole profession, civil and natural law proclaim such exercise unjust."

It is impossible to deny the ingenuity of the argument here given, identical with that ever since employed by the advocates of exclusive trade societies: that the interest of the many—*i.e.* the many of the same trade—is to be preferred to the interest of one. A single workman, by accepting wages below the tariff, or by working too vigorously, may lead to a change prejudicial to the whole trade. Of course the answer is that the still greater number, the public at large, are left out of view altogether. If the interests of a thousand are to overbalance those of one, still more must the interests of hundreds of thousands or of millions overbalance those of thousands.

Social Effects of Private Monopolies.—Let it be understood, then, in the clearest way, that whosoever tries to raise his own wages by preventing other persons from working at his trade, and thus makes his own kind of labour scarce, attempts to levy contributions from other people. It is simply a case of private taxation. In the early Norman times it was not uncommon for the small seaport towns to impose customs duties of their own upon goods imported, the proceeds being applied to the advantage of the town. One of the first results of improved government was the abolition of such exclusive imposts. Whatever duties were levied were to go to the king, who was supposed to expend them for the benefit of the whole community.

Those who pay the private duties levied by exclusive trades are the consumers of the goods made by the trade. High wages for hat-makers simply mean high prices of hats, and so much out of the pockets of hat-wearers. Or, as in consequence of expense the hat-wearers will probably wear fewer hats, it means less convenience to them. We ought not to look at such subjects from a class point of view, and in economics at any rate should regard all men as brothers. But it cannot escape attention that, as by far the larger number of hat-wearers are workmen, a very large part of the tax in any case falls upon brother workmen. In this particular case the harm done may not be considerable, but in the case of other trades it certainly is. Nothing, for instance, can be more injurious to the poorer classes than any artificial restrictions in the building trades tending to raise the cost of building, or to impede the introduction of improvements in bricklaying and the other building arts. The effect is peculiarly injurious, because it places great obstacles in the way of any attempt to produce really good new dwellings for the working classes. There are always quantities of old houses and buildings of various sorts which can be let as lodgings at a rate below that at which it is possible to build good new ones. The result is either that very inferior cheap houses must be built, or the more expensive model dwellings fall practically to a better-paid class. The general effect is to make really wholesome houses a luxury for the wealthier classes, while the residuum have to herd together between whatever walls they can find.

Of course it may be said that to some extent unionists raise their wages at the cost of the wealthy classes. Beautifully-printed books, for instance, are seldom purchased except by book-fanciers, and other well-to-do people. Hence, if high wages could be maintained in the high-class printing houses, the extra cost would come, not out of the employer's funds, but out of the spare cash of the book-buyers. Little harm would be done in this particular case, because such bibliomaniacs actually aim at finding scarce and costly books, and buy in preference those books which are printed in small numbers. But anything which tends to raise the price of printing in general has the very pernicious effect of hindering the diffusion of knowledge among the people.

Nor is the injury to their fellow-workmen by exclusive trades unionists solely produced by this raising of cost directly. As is ingeniously pointed out by Professor Alfred Marshall in his *Economics of Industry* (pp. 206-7), several trades usually act together in the production of any important commodity. Thus bricklayers, stone-masons, carpenters, plasterers, slaters, painters, common labourers, and various minor trades, are all concerned in the production of a house. If, then, any one of these trades, say plasterers, could by combination seriously raise their wages, and thus add to the cost of the house, the effect would be to diminish the demand for such houses, and to lessen the wages of the other trades concerned. Each trade which maintains a strict union is, in fact, striving to secure an unfair share of the public expenditure. Though workmen, in respect of belonging to the same social class, may try to persuade themselves that their interests are identical, this is not really the case. They are and must be competitors, and every rise of wages which one body secures by mere exclusive combination represents a certain amount, sometimes a large amount, of injury to the other bodies of workmen. We must further take into account the consideration that by raising barriers around trades, and preventing the surplus labour of one from finding employment in another, there is a general decrease of producing power. On the whole, then, we conclude that it is quite impossible for trades unions in general to effect any permanent increase of wages, and that success in maintaining exclusive monopolies leads to great loss and injury to the community in general.

There would be a certain fairness in the establishment of monopolies if all trades were equally able to combine and tax each other. The result would of course be very absurd and very pernicious, but it would be equal. As a matter of fact, however, those who most need combination to better their fortunes are just those who are the least able to carry it out. As in so many other walks of life, to him that hath shall be given. A small body of skilled men are able in some cases to form a nearly complete and exclusive society, and by the restriction of apprentices to hold the "mystery" as their private property. This power would doubtless be much more used were it not controlled by the competition of foreign producers. Where goods are very portable in proportion to value, it is obviously impossible for any mere trade society to prevent the substitution of foreign productions. There are certain trades, however, which are concerned either with very heavy, bulky goods, or else with work which must be performed upon the spot. Bricks, for instance, of which 1000 may be had for a little more than twenty shillings, are usually made in close proximity to the buildings of which they are to form part. In any case, they cannot be concealed, and thus brickmakers are (or were) able to exercise a close supervision over the sources of supply. Accordingly, the brickmakers of Manchester actually succeeded for a length of time in maintaining the rule that no bricks made beyond four miles of Manchester should be brought into that city. House-carpenters formerly enjoyed the advantage of making all the woodwork of a house upon the spot. A close union could then by a strike entirely stop the progress of the building. The advance in the use of wood-working machinery, and the possibility of importing foreign machine-made window-frames and doors, has somewhat diminished this advantage. But the plasterers still have the master builders at their mercy; for, though a few mouldings and casts may be made elsewhere, the bulk of the plasterer's work must be done actually upon the walls and ceilings of the house *in situ*. In countries where wooden houses are chiefly used, these may be bought and carried piecemeal for erection on any spot; but those who prefer to dwell in brick, stone, and plaster dwellings must continue for the present to be more or less at the mercy of the building trades.

Such being the facts with regard to exclusive trade monopolies, what is the attitude which the State should maintain towards them? Economists have almost unanimously condemned such trade societies. Adam Smith refers in a condemnatory tone to the exclusive privileges of corporations, and all laws which restrain in particular employments the competition to a smaller number than might otherwise go into them. They are, he thought, a sort of enlarged monopoly, and might keep the market price of particular commodities above the natural price, maintaining both the wages of labour, and, as he correctly adds, the profits of stock employed about them, somewhat above their natural rate.[1]

J. S. Mill, after expressing some opinions in which I cannot coincide, has added[2] the following striking passage, which cannot be too much read:—

"If the present state of the general habits of the people were to remain for ever unimproved, these partial combinations, in so far as they do succeed in keeping up the wages of any trade by limiting its numbers might be looked upon as simply intrenching round a particular spot against the inroads of over-population, and making their wages depend upon their own rate of increase, instead of depending on that of a more reckless and improvident class than themselves. The time, however, is past when the friends of human improvement can look with complacency on the attempts of small sections of the community, whether belonging to the labouring or any other class, to organise a separate

[1] *Wealth of Nations*, Book I. chap. vii.

[2] *Principles of Political Economy*, Book II. chap. xiv. sec. 6.

class interest in antagonism to the general body of labourers."

Professor Fawcett also is not less emphatic in protesting against such monopolies. He says:[1]—"If trades unions are permitted to prevent this free passage of labour from one employment to another, wages may permanently maintain an artificial advance; but trades unions can only exert such an influence by resorting to a social tyranny, which is in every sense illegal and unjustifiable." But it is, of course, one thing to protest in theory; it is another to interfere by force of law. A brief consideration of the history of the Combination Laws will show how hopeless is the attempt to prevent trade confederacies by direct prohibition.

The Combination Laws.—In view of the economic principles considered above, What is the duty of the legislator? Monopoly in any trade is against the public interest. Ought not the lawgiver, then, simply to prohibit societies which tend towards such monopoly? and ought they not to carry out the law with all "the resources of civilisation"? There are, however, two reasons against such forcible suppression: in the first place, it is impracticable and impossible; in the second place, if possible, it would suppress with much evil many germs of good. As to the first point, which might seem decisive of the question, we have the evidence of long experience. Our grandfathers and great grandfathers, not to speak of earlier ancestors, did their best to crush all societies of working men, and ignominious was their failure. Are we likely to succeed better when

[1] *Manual of Political Economy*, 2d ed., p. 2.

the working-class order has become immensely increased in numbers, and increased almost equally in intelligence, organisation, wealth, and general resources?

Regard to space will not allow of my citing fully the evidence which conclusively proved the failure of the restrictive legislation. The Combination Laws begin with that quaint Act of the 33 Edward I. (stat. 2, 1304),—"Who be conspirators and who be champertors." This curious law is a definition only, not an enactment. "Conspirators," it says, "be they that do confeder or bind themselves by oath, covenant, or other alliance, that every of them shall aid and bear the other falsely and maliciously to indite," etc. It seems to have been thought quite sufficient to define who were conspirators; the rest went without saying.

The subsequent long series of Combination Laws, about thirty-five in number, are fully recapitulated in the first section of the 5 Geo. IV. cap. 95, which swept them away so far as they rendered it illegal for workmen to meet together to deliberate and agree upon the terms and wages for which they should labour. Most of these Acts related only to particular trades; thus the "journeymen tailors within the weekly bills of mortality" came under the care of the Legislature in the 7 Geo. I. and the 8 Geo. III.; the better regulation of the linen and hempen manufactures was provided for in the 3 Geo. III., and so forth. Finding, however, in 1800, that in spite of the many complicated enactments then in force strikes and combinations were still rampant, the Legislature directed a final blow against workmen's associations in the 39 and 40 Geo. III. cap. 106. By this thoroughgoing law all agreements between journeymen and workmen for obtaining advances of wages, reductions of hours of labour, or any other changes in the conditions of work, were declared illegal; persons entering into such agreements could be convicted summarily by two justices of the peace, and committed to prison for two months. A like penalty was imposed upon all who should, by giving money, by persuasion, intimidation, or otherwise, prevent any unhired workman from hiring himself, or any hired workman from continuing in his employ, and so forth. But, as Mr. Longe remarks, in his interesting sketch of this legislation [1]—"This elaborate attempt on the part of the Legislature to prevent 'strikes' was its last. Experience soon showed that such laws were not only useless, but pernicious." This *experience* is sufficiently detailed in various parts of the excellent volume referred to. The effect of such laws was not to suppress societies, but to render them secret conspiracies. Very often clubs, simulating the character of friendly societies in public, acted as trade societies in private. Some societies boldly defied the law, especially the formidable union of the Liverpool shipwrights. According to Mr. Philip Rathbone's report on the Liverpool trade societies, these bold shipwrights used to range about the town carrying a loaded cannon with them.

There were prosecutions from time to time. In 1805 three linen weavers of Knaresborough were sent to gaol for three months, one of them for simply carrying a letter to York requesting assistance. Mr. George Howell specifies a good many other cases (pp. 121-124), especially a notable one in Lancashire in 1818, in which

[1] *Report on Trades Societies:* Social Science Association, 1860, p. 345.

a trade union deputy was sent to prison for twelve months, although his own employer gave evidence in his favour, and said that he had himself suggested the resolutions carried at the illegal meeting of workmen. A most telling fact is that in some cases the masters declared to their men their intention not to appeal to the Combination Laws, and more peaceful relations between the parties then ensued. The writer of the admirable anonymous tract "On Combinations of Trades," published in 1831, asserts that the general conviction of the injustice and impolicy of these laws had produced a disinclination on the part both of masters and justices to put them in force unless in seasons of disturbance, when they were administered for other purposes. But we need hardly resort to secondary evidence when we find that a Committee of the House of Commons declared "that the Act of the 39 and 40 of his present Majesty, for settling disputes between masters and workmen engaged in the cotton manufacture in England, has not produced the good effects that were expected from it."[1]

It was upon such grounds of distinct experience, rather than upon any theory of freedom of trade, that Parliament in 1824, led mainly by the lamented Huskisson, swept those mistaken laws away. The act was inevitable, and yet it was momentous; for it has led to the growth of the many great societies which now exist and, as many people think, oppress industry. It is requisite from time to time to remind one generation of the experience which led a former generation to important legislative actions.

[1] *Journals of the House of Commons*, 28th March 1804, vol. lix. p. 187.

The Legislation of Trades Unions.—It is very desirable that the public, especially the working-class public, should always bear in mind exactly what was the intention and effect of the Trades Union Acts of 1871 and 1876, which enabled trades societies to be registered and to obtain legal facilities equivalent to those enjoyed by registered friendly societies. The matter is a technical one, of no real importance in principle, but the change made in the law is liable to be misconstrued into an approval by the State of trade combinations. Previous to the passing of the above-named Acts, trades societies, being deemed illegal in respect of acting in restraint of trade, were excluded from registration under the Friendly Societies Act (18 and 19 Vict. cap. 63, sec. 44). This Act granted special benefits as regards security of property and settlement of disputes to any societies established for certain specified purposes, and in certain cases "for any purpose which is not illegal." But then it must be remembered that exclusion from this Act was only exclusion from special facilities. The members did not lose their ordinary legal rights, and, if the funds of the society were made away with, could proceed under the ordinary law, provided, indeed, that no unlawful acts or purposes in restraint of trade could be proved against the union.

But as in modern times governments could not venture to prevent the existence of associations of all kinds, there arose gradually the anomaly of societies allowed to exist, and yet deprived of any means of putting the law into effective operation. Lawyers would probably be the first to allow that the law of partnership, whether theoretically good or not, was practically inapplicable to societies whose rates of subscription were counted in shillings or pence. The expense of proceedings and the difficulty of proving ownership in common funds was such as to amount to practical refusal of justice, and several scandalous cases occurred in which the embezzlement of the funds of unions was thus allowed to go unpunished. The state of the law was such as to promote and encourage fraud and injustice. There was no sense in trying to discourage unions by indirect means, which did not prevent their formation, but which obliged the members either to suffer from fraud or else to resort to violent means of redress, such as is practised upon "welchers" at a race meeting.

Under the present state of the law, however (Trades Union Acts, 1871 and 1876), great facilities are enjoyed by unions. They can hold land and other property in the names of trustees, and can carry on all legal proceedings in the trustees' names. They have remedy on summary conviction for any fraud or illegality on the part of their officers. Members' property in the union funds can be transmitted at death without a will, and various other facilities are enjoyed, as described in the Report of the Chief Registrar of Friendly Societies, 1877, p. 32. It is remarkable, however, that very few trades societies have availed themselves of these advantages, the number in 1878 being only 177, compared with 17,776 registered societies of other kinds. Possibly the necessity of registering the rules has had a deterrent influence in some cases.

It is a matter worthy of consideration, however, whether the Legislature ought not finally to give up its jealousy of associative action, by recognising in law courts every society of whose existence formal evidence can be given. The law has come, in fact, very nearly to this point. The Friendly Societies Act of 1855 (18 and 19 Vict. cap. 63, sec. 9) gave power to a Secretary of State to name "additional purposes" to which the powers and facilities of the Act might be extended. Under this, and the like provisions in subsequent Acts (see the Consolidation Act of 1875, 38 and 39 Vict. cap. 60, sec. 8 [5]), additions have been made. In January 1878 societies guaranteeing the performance of their duties by officers of friendly societies were allowed to be registered. In April of the same year societies for playing the game of quoits were approved by the Treasury; and finally, in July 1878, there was made the sweeping addition of societies for the promotion of literature, science, and the fine arts. All societies "for any charitable or benevolent purpose" had been previously eligible for registration. Now these terms are so wide and vague as to comprehend almost every purpose for which associations, not for trading purposes, could be formed. The public appear to be generally ignorant of these facilities, and the number of registrations under the additional powers is very limited. The point of most interest to us here is that the existence of such comprehensive definitions disposes of the idea that the Legislature, in allowing the registration of trade societies, gave any kind of special approval or facility to them.

The Good and Evil of Strikes.—I have adopted, in the first chapter, the doctrine that in social as in physical matters we must be guided by experience—direct specific experience if possible. But nothing is more necessary than to bear in mind how impossible it is in some cases to interpret experience with certainty. Especially is this the case as regards the effects of strikes. Of these we have indeed had ample experience. Hardly can we take up any newspaper without meeting accounts of strikes, small or large, in some parts of the country. In the Trades Societies' Report of the Social Science Association we have minute details of some of the most celebrated and prolonged strikes—such as that of Preston in 1853, the Yorkshire coal strike of 1858, or the building trades strike in London in 1859-60. The origin and results of many strikes are also investigated in the evidence taken by the Trades Union Commission of 1867. Any one who wishes to appreciate fully the difference of opinions which may be held on this subject should compare the optimist view of Mr. George Howell in his important article on "Strikes: their Cost and Results," in *Fraser's Magazine* for December 1879, with the somewhat pessimist conclusions derived by Mr. G. P. Bevan from his very careful and elaborate statistical inquiries, as given in the *Statistical Journal* for March 1880, vol. xliii. pp. 35-54.

Primâ facie, indeed, we might take the recurrence of strikes as evidence of their success; for it is hardly to be supposed that the workmen so seriously concerned would venture on new strikes unless they were satisfied that advantage was derived by themselves or other workmen from previous strikes. It would seem, in short, as if we had the direct specific experience needed to settle the matter. A little consideration, however, will show that this is one of the cases where the whole difficulty lies in interpreting experience. In a certain proportion of strikes no doubt the strikers do really succeed in gaining what they demand; and more than this, other workmen of the same trade often profit from a corresponding rise of wages conceded in consequence by their employers. It may also be argued that, since workmen acquired the liberty of striking at discretion, their wages have been greatly advanced,—a fact which will not be disputed. But it is altogether a different matter to infer that because increased wages have been attained the strikes are the cause of attainment. This argument is essentially one of the kind *post hoc, ergo propter hoc*—a kind of argument more often fallacious than sound. We must remember that many other causes have been in operation tending towards the increase of earnings. Free trade has made the world our customers; invention has proceeded by leaps and bounds; the power of coal has been brought to the assistance of human labour; the capital of employers has grown vastly; the productive powers of machinery have been multiplied time after time. Moreover, great changes have taken place in the purchasing power of money. We should have to allow for these and not a few other causes before we could really infer that any definite rise of wages is due to a strike. In view of this multiplicity of causes, in fact, the method of direct experience fails.

The last chance of a verdict conclusively in favour of strikes is removed when we remember that the general rise of wages allowed by statists to have occurred is by no means confined to trades which are united and addicted to striking, but extends more or less distinctly to all classes of employees. Many extensive groups of workers, such as mercantile and bank clerks, Government clerks and officials, post-office employees, policemen, soldiers, and so forth, have all attained distinct and, what is more, permanent advances of salary, without anything to be called striking. Still more remarkably is this the case with domestic servants, an exceedingly numerous class of persons, quite devoid of organisation, and often of an age and character little suited, it might be thought, to enforce concession. Yet, by the natural operation of the laws of supply and demand, and by their own good sense, these employees have been greatly advanced in earnings and other advantages. So far as regards employments free from fluctuations of trade, the evidence tends to show conclusively the uselessness and harm of strikes.

The case, no doubt, is somewhat different where there are violent oscillations of activity and depression, as in the coal and iron trades especially. It is of such trades, in all probability, that Professor Fawcett was thinking when he said—"I cannot, after great deliberation, resist the conclusion, that such a power of combination may secure to the labourers higher wages in certain special states of trade." It is difficult indeed to deny that in a sudden improvement of trade a strike or the threat of a strike will occasionally induce masters to raise wages with a promptitude otherwise not to be expected. But the reverse process is witnessed when the wave begins to recede: the masters having promptly advanced wages determine to reduce them with like promptitude, whereas the men, convinced of the efficacy of strikes, resist when the circumstances are all against them. Nothing is clearer than that in a time of falling demand strikes must fail. They often form, indeed, the opportunity—as in the disastrous strike at Cyfartha—for employers to close works which they might otherwise have felt bound to carry on at some risk of loss.

So difficult, or rather impossible, is it to distinguish the cases in which strikes must inflict great loss and disappointment and those in which they may yield at least apparent success, that the economist incurs grave responsibility in expressing approval of any strikes. As well commend gambling because there are occasions when the gambler gains, as commend striking because "in certain special states of trade" it may be successful. The only true system of striking is for every man to strike individually when he has an undoubted opportunity of bettering his position.

Professional Trades Unions.—During the long and bitter controversies which have been waged on the Trades Union question, no argument has been found more telling on the side of the unions than the *tu quoque* retort. Trades unions, it is said, are not confined to handicraftsmen. The legal and medical professions understand equally well the virtue of combination. The Inns of Court, the Colleges of Surgeons and Physicians, and suchlike bodies, are but exclusive trade societies of the upper classes. The very name *college* implies as much, collegium (*con*, together; and *legere*, to gather) being, in fact, the Latin equivalent of association, or guild. It is only in late years that the name, college, has become specialised to associations of teachers, and thence applied to mere schools for boys and girls.

This *tu quoque* argument is so far true that the only possible way of meeting it is to admit its substantial truth. There can be no doubt whatever that both the legal and medical professions are pervaded by strong "professional" feelings, and that under the euphemism of "professional etiquette," they are governed by elaborate systems of social terrorism. Nobody could possibly have followed the several steps of the struggle concerning the admission of women to the practice of medicine, especially the debates and votes on the subject in the Convocation of the London University, without feeling that it was simply a trade question. As to the Inns of Court, venerable as they are in respect of age—having been founded at various dates between 1310 and 1520—they were but lately trades unions in an advanced stage of degeneration, and they are not very much better now. Entry was obtained by the mere form of eating dinners in the public hall, and the paying of certain substantial fees. The true genius of the trades union is shown in the jealous care with which the barristers exclude solicitors, the exclusion being in former years absolutely, and in the present day sufficiently, complete. The same spirit is also evinced in the vexatious restrictions regarding circuits. Every circuit mess is a separate union, election to which is practically compulsory. Having joined one mess, the barrister is confined to it, and must refuse work from other circuits except at "special rates."

But while it is impossible not to admit that the bodies referred to are trades unions of a well-marked type in some respects, they are strongly distinguished from the handicraft unions in other important respects. In the first place, no attempt is made at limiting the numbers of members. Every respectable man who brings the requisite fees and goes through the proper forms, is admitted almost without exception. So much is this the case in the Inns of Court, that the nominal barristers-at-law are perhaps two or three times as numerous as those barristers who really practise with success. Even in the medical profession, where entry is now barred by stiff examination, as well as by costly education and not inconsiderable fees, the number who qualify for practice is distinctly in excess of those who adhere to the profession and eventually succeed. The danger, if anything, lies in the direction of too free admission, and the temptation is always on the side of relaxing every condition except the payment of fees.

Again, within these professional bodies there is no trace of socialistic tendency. On the contrary, the keenest possible competition is the rule. Successful barristers and physicians make their £10,000 or £15,000 a year; but, instead of meeting with obloquy and opposition from their less successful brothers, they are the objects of admiration and esteem. Thus the life of an eminent professional man becomes one unceasing round of severe labour; his talent and experience are multiplied in utility to the highest possible degree, not without reward to himself, but with still greater benefit to a public who need skilful assistance. In the case of the bar, this unlimited competition tends perhaps to run into excess and abuse; but as regards the medical profession, I am unable to see any evil in the present system, the avenue to distinction and success usually lying through long-continued gratuitous services at hospitals, or a distinguished career as a public teacher of the healing art.

There is, too, a third condition which strongly distinguishes professional from handicraft unions, namely, the exaction in the present day of a more or less severe entrance examination. Corporations, according to J.-B. Say, have never really guaranteed the quality of the goods which they produce. It would not be practicable for the College of Surgeons to guarantee continuously the excellence of the services rendered by their members. But, so far as entrance examinations are concerned, there is little ground of complaint at present. As to the expediency of some State regulation of the medical and legal professions, no serious difference of opinion can exist. Medical advice is obviously a thing of which an ordinary patient is incapable of judging; it clearly falls, therefore, under the category of commodities which may be inspected by State officers. Clearly, too, the intention of the Legislature has always been to secure the efficiency of practitioners. Thus, shortly before the establishment of the College of Physicians, we find that an Act was passed (3 Henry VIII. cap. 11), providing that no one should take upon him, "to exercise and occupy" as a physician or surgeon in London, unless he had been admitted by the Bishop of London or the Dean of St. Paul's. These eminent ecclesiastics were not themselves to be the judges of efficiency, but were to call unto them four doctors of physic, and "for surgery, other expert persons in that faculty, and for the first examination such as they shall think convenient, and afterward alway four of them that have been so approved." In other parts of the country the bishop of the diocese, or the vicar-general, was to be the licensing authority. The method of examination, then, was established by law more than 350 years ago. From time to time, no doubt, in spite of renewed legislation, the examinations fell into abeyance, or were little more than nominal.

In recent years, it need hardly be said, the practice and the art of examination have made rapid progress. Examinations have become the sole mode of entry, not only into the medical profession, the lower branch of the law, the civil service, the army and navy, and even the church, but many other bodies of professional men have taken steps in the like direction. A Surveyors' Institute has just been created, entry to which will be eventually confined to successful examinees. The Institute of Actuaries, the Bankers' Institute, and the Society of Chartered Accountants, have also established systems of examination. It is even proposed, by means of an Act for the registration of teachers, to make some kind of examination test a legal qualification for all teachers in secondary schools.

So long as entrance examinations are of a *bonâ fide* character, there is no analogy between such chartered bodies and mere trades unions. No trade society has in recent times made even the pretence of exacting a test of proficiency. In former days the apprentice, before he could be admitted to act as journeyman, was required to exhibit his *chef d'œuvre* as a specimen of his skill. I am not aware that any such test is ever applied now. The applicant for admission to a modern trades union must indeed satisfy the society that he is capable of earning the usual wages, but this is only in order that his employment may not tend to make a precedent for admitting lower rates of wages. So good a witness as Mr. G. J. Holyoake says (*History of Co-operation*, vol. ii. p. 262)—"Now, a man being a unionist, is no guarantee to any one that he will not scamp his work, or do the least for the most he can get. . . . A trades-union council are not leaders of art in industry; they are, with a few exceptions, mere connoisseurs in strikes. All a union does is to strike against low wages, they never strike against doing bad work." It is indeed remarkable that with their extensive funds, widespread organisation, and trade-knowledge, hardly any union has attempted to carry on industry itself. They confine themselves to criticism and opposition. Even their funds are deposited in banks or other ordinary modes of investment, and find their way round into the hands of capitalists, perhaps their own obnoxious employers. In spite of the evils and horrors of "capitalism," the workmen can find no way of using their own capital but such as put it into the hands of their supposed enemies.

There can be no doubt that the system of examinations will go on and prosper, and that we have not yet seen the end of the movement towards the incorporation of professions. There can, however, be equally little doubt that the public and the Legislature must keep a vigilant eye on all such bodies, and must without scruple reform them as soon as ever they fall away from their original good purpose.

Principle of Degeneration of Associations.—In attempting to forecast the future of trade societies, it is indispensable to take account of what I may call the *principle of degeneration*, which applies to all associations of men. Every society which has perpetual succession is subject to a tendency to fall away from its original purposes. Although formed in the first instance by persons having a definite object in view, the society subsequently becomes a distinct entity. It acquires reputation and power; it often collects endowments and acquires vested interests of various kinds. By degrees those who act as officers are drawn aside by their private interests, and there is no setting a limit to the possible divergence of the institution from the intentions of its founders.

It is hardy requisite to illustrate this statement; instances of degeneration pour upon us. St. Katharine's Hospital in Regent's Park, the city companies, sundry ancient colleges before their reformation, the Inns of Court, as they were not long ago, are sufficient instances. The change, however, is not always correctly described as degeneration; though diverging from its original purpose, a society often develops into something of unexpected utility. A small benefaction for the erection of a hospital leads to the creation of a great medical and scientific school. A convivial club of a score of members grows into the greatest of learned societies. By far the most singular of such transformations, however, is that of the Freemasons' societies.

The Freemasons' lodges were originally simple trade societies of the skilful builders who in the Middle Ages raised our grand cathedrals and our beautiful parish churches. A lodge was established at York as early as A.D. 926, and the order is said to have been introduced into England some centuries before, perhaps in 674. However that may be, the societies retained their distinctive trade character throughout the Middle Ages, as we learn incidentally from the Act 3 Henry VI. cap. 1, against masons who "confederate themselves in chapiters and assemblies." That great builder, William of Wykeham, was at one time Grand Master, and as late as 1666 Sir Christopher Wren was elected deputy grand-master, in recognition of his skill as an architect and builder. Subsequently the order has become entirely disconnected from the building trade, and while ever prospering has adopted philanthropic or social purposes. The square and compasses, once the actual implements of its members, are now mere mystic symbols.

The bearing of this principle of degeneration on our subject is very evident. The existing great trade societies only need to be let alone and they will probably degenerate from their original trade purposes. But inasmuch as those trade purposes were against the public good, the process of degeneration will probably bring them more nearly into consonance with public interests. What were, under the Combination Laws, mere midnight conspiracies, are developing and will develop into widespread philanthropic bodies, headed by members of Parliament, meeting in large halls before a table full of reporters, gradually giving up their selfish and mistaken ideas. No one could have read the proceedings of the recent Trades Union Congress in London without feeling that recent wise legislation was bearing good fruit. Instead of machine-breakers and midnight conspirators, the working-men met as the members of a parliament to discuss the means and ends of legislation with dignity and propriety at least equal to that recently exhibited at St. Stephen's. No longer entirely devoted to the pet fallacies and interests of their order, their deliberations touch many of the most important social questions of the day. The more extensive the federations of trades which thus meet in peaceful conference, the more wide and generous must of necessity become their views. Enjoying all the rights and performing all the duties of the English citizen, the trades unionist will before long cease his exclusive strife against his true ally, his wealthy employer. It is impossible not to accept the general views of Mr. Henry Crompton, that as working-men gradually acquire their full rights, their leaders will turn to the noble task of impressing upon them the duties of citizenship.

CHAPTER V

THE LAW OF INDUSTRIAL CONSPIRACY

THERE is no part of the law relating to labour which has been debated with more bitterness than that touching the doctrine of conspiracy. Until quite recent years the common law gave power to the judges, or they at any rate assumed the power, to treat any combination of labourers aiming at the increase of wages as a conspiracy against the public weal, an attempt at public mischief, which could be punished as a misdemeanour by fine and imprisonment. The celebrated case of the Dorsetshire labourers in the year 1834 was an instance of the exercise of this somewhat arbitrary power. The common law has now been defined and restricted, if not almost abrogated, by the Conspiracy and Protection of Property Act, 1875, which in the 3d section enacts that an agreement or combination by two or more persons to do or procure to be done any act in contemplation or furtherance of a trade dispute between employers and workmen shall not be indictable as a conspiracy if such act committed by one person would not be punishable as a crime. But as other parts of the same section and the same Act continue or impose special penalties in the case of proceedings involving conspiracy, some unionists are still dissatisfied at the state of the law. They regard these penalties as being still specially aimed at combinations of working-men, as relics, in fact, of past mistaken class legislation, and it is seriously urged that the offence of conspiracy should be entirely abolished as regards labour questions. It is not superfluous, therefore, to inquire into the grounds of the law of conspiracy.

What is Conspiracy?—That confident but often mistaken economist MacCulloch has touched the point of the matter when he says, in his little treatise on Wages (2d ed. p. 90): "A criminal act cannot be generated by the mere multiplication of acts that are perfectly innocent." This statement may be true as it stands, but it has no reference to conspiracy. To ask for more wages is a perfectly legal act, and if a thousand men were to be struck independently with a wish for higher wages, and were to go and ask separately, there would be no conspiracy in the matter. But, if a number of men meet together and agree jointly to ask for more, and then persuade others to do likewise, it is not a mere multiplication of requests; it is that *plus* an agreement and an organised arrangement. The difference is even greater than this: the act becomes different in nature by reason of the concert and the purpose implied in that concert.

It is, for example, a perfectly legal action to walk along a highway, and no multiplication of such acts in the ordinary course of life or business can render them illegal. If so many men happened some day to want to walk through Throgmorton Street that the street became entirely blocked up, there would still be no legal offence. The concourse would be fortuitous, and each man would be simply exercising his legal right under difficulties. But if a number of men were to agree together that they would walk up and down Throgmorton Street on a particular day, the complexion of the act would be entirely changed. The act is no doubt physically the same; but, being accompanied with the knowledge that other people would do the same, and that a block would be occasioned, there would be reason to presume some special purpose, as, for instance, the obstructing the business of the Stock Exchange, or occasioning alarm, perhaps panic, in the city. The act would be illegal in respect of the intention to block up the Queen's highway, and it would be further illegal in respect of a special purpose, which, though not illegal in itself, might be illegal if sought by means of combination.

Surely it cannot escape attention that many of the industrial and other ordinary arrangements of society entirely hang upon the tacit assumption that individuals will act as individuals, pursuing independent and usual courses of action. A footpath, an omnibus, a railway train, is calculated only for the ordinary average traffic. A banker's business entirely depends upon the presumption that, while some customers are drawing out, others will be paying money in. There is no bank in the country which could stand a run on the part of a considerable number of its depositors. But, according to the theory of probabilities, it is practically impossible that such a sudden concurrence of demands should take place really by accident; the mere occurrence of such a run would be sufficient evidence of a common cause, which might be merely a false rumour, or it might be a conspiracy of depositors to ruin the bank. Now, it must be quite apparent that any agreement between bank depositors to draw out money in order to overthrow a bank is a totally different thing from drawing out in the ordinary course of business, and is, in fact, a serious matter.

It must be easy to see that there is hardly one of the ordinary arrangements of trade which may not be entirely upset by concerted action. The bakers and butchers might starve us out; the cab proprietors might refuse to carry us away; innkeepers might decline to harbour us; our neighbours might tacitly avoid assisting us. No man's life would be safe if unlimited "Boycotting" were regarded as legal.

Industrial Treason.—It must be apparent, too, that this subject assumes by degrees higher importance as the organisation of society becomes more complex and delicate, and the condensation of population greater. London might be reduced to starvation and anarchy by a well-devised combination among a few thousands of men. When we depend for water upon one organisation, for light upon another, for food upon railways and a long series of middlemen, the state of things is very different from that of the old-fashioned house with a well in the back-yard, and plenty of candles, salt-meat, and groceries in the store-room.

It seems to me to be quite impossible, then, to suppose that the law of conspiracy can be entirely repealed. Such entire abrogation would enable a handful, or at most a few thousands, of men, by legal means, to coerce the community to any extent, and, in the absence of concession, to inflict immeasurable injury. It is still a serious crime to purchase arms and to organise and drill a body of men in order to oppose the State, or any of its authorities. Treason is still an offence in the Statute-Book. But so all-powerful has the English Government become in recent times by the inventions of science and the improvements of organisation, that little harm is to be feared from this antiquated kind of treason. But I venture to think that a great strike, if carried sufficiently far, might assume the character of social treason. As in the case of the great railway strike in the United States in 1877, it might bring society to a dead lock. If ten thousand Yorkshiremen were to march upon London, with the very best arms they could muster, the Government would probably surround and capture them in twenty-four hours by the aid of railways and telegraphs. But if ten thousand railway men were to form a conspiracy to obstruct and destroy the railways and telegraphs of the kingdom, they would create infinitely greater alarm and injury, and would be checked with far greater difficulty. It is thus highly needful to bear in mind how the more delicate and elaborate arrangements of modern society have caused a change in the bearing of social dangers.

In accordance, however, with what has been said before, it is one thing to hold that there must exist the offence of conspiracy, and another thing to say that any particular kind of conspiracy should be punished. Conspiracy is especially a question of degree, varying in several ways, as regards the number of persons involved, the consciousness of common intention on their part, and the innocence or noxiousness of the purpose aimed at. One end of the scale is formed by some case in which thousands of men intentionally injure society in a manner which might lead to death, distress, and harm incalculable. At the other end of the scale we may place the case of a few workmen talking over together the state of trade and their own condition, and agreeing unanimously that they must ask for more wages. Nothing can be easily conceived more innocent, if not praiseworthy, than the latter action; few things more blamable than the former. It is, therefore, the extreme vagueness and graduation of the act of conspiracy which constitutes the difficulty. This was surmounted in the old common law, if, indeed, surmounted at all, by leaving it to the discretion of the judges only to apply the law where the interests of society required it. But even judges are not always perfectly discreet; and the sentence of seven years' transportation passed upon the Dorsetshire labourers for a mere strike, involving nothing which we should now esteem criminal, not unnaturally created intense indignation throughout the country.

The Present Law.—I venture to hold, therefore, that the Conspiracy and Protection of Property Act of 1875 was drawn upon the proper lines. It endeavoured to discriminate between such acts of conspiracy as are and are not highly noxious to society. Thus any breach of contract involving failure of the water and gas supplies of towns or other places is rendered punishable with imprisonment for three months, under the fourth section. The next section is a much more elastic one, inflicting like punishment "where any person wilfully and maliciously breaks a contract of service or of hiring, knowing or having reasonable cause to believe that the probable consequences of his so doing, either alone or in combination with others, will be to endanger human life, or cause serious bodily injury, or to expose valuable property whether real or personal to destruction or serious injury." The seventh section, again, enacts special penalties for any person convicted of intimidating, annoying, or watching another person, with a view to compel him to do or abstain from doing any act which such person has a legal right to do or abstain from doing. It has been frequently urged, indeed, that these special penalties are invidious. If the acts of intimidation and annoyance are illegal, why should they not be left to be dealt with by the general law? But here again is false analogy; to shake your fist at a man is no doubt the same physical act whether done in momentary anger or as part of an extensive concerted system of actions. But it may have vastly greater significance and importance in the latter than the former case. The law must always look to the real character of the action, not to the mere outward manifestation. The whole of the criminal law may be said to consist of special penalties for special acts according to their social noxiousness. Forgery is only one mode of fraud, but being peculiarly dangerous to society is punished with special severity. To break into a house is the same act physically whether done by day or by night; but being more alarming and injurious in the latter case is treated as the special crime of burglary, and punished with greater severity. Having regard now to the peculiar and in fact extraordinary powers which combinations of men acting well together may acquire, it is not at all unnatural that any illegal acts which they commit should need repression under a special law adapted to the circumstances.

Industrial Emergency.—One point of much importance concerning the Conspiracy and Protection of Property Act is that it only punishes conduct leading to injury of property, loss of life, etc., when it involves breach of contract. Thus, if a body of workmen employed in water or gas works leave in a body at the expiration of their agreement, they commit no offence, be the consequences to the community what they may. This seems to be reasonable enough, because they act within the terms of their engagement, and the community through their servants, the water and gas companies, ought to take care of themselves. But we can easily conceive conjunctures to arise in which perfectly legal action may inflict the highest injury on society. If any very large proportion of the colliers of the kingdom, for instance, were to leave work, even after due legal notice, they might bring the industry of the country to a standstill. Not only industry, indeed, but the sustenance and health of millions of their fellow-citizens would be imperilled.

Necessity knows no law, and the essence of illegality is injury to other people. I conceive, therefore, that in repealing the old common law of conspiracy as regards industrial disputes the Act in question has opened up at least the possibility of injurious actions for which no legal remedy is provided. Of course if such extreme cases could not occur there would be no good in providing against them, which is perhaps the motive of the repeal referred to. But then the federated societies of colliers have repeatedly proposed to resort to a universal strike; and ten years ago, though they never went to such an extreme length, they inflicted much harm upon the industry of the country, and eventually upon themselves, by restricting the output of coal. So entirely has coal now become the motive-force of all industry, the source of maintenance, that a really complete strike of colliers would place the country in a state of siege as completely as Paris was so placed by the German armies. We cannot seriously contemplate the idea of a coalless and foodless nation, perishing because some quarter of a million of colliers refuse to work. Yet a strike of only a few weeks would reduce the country to a state of which we have no present idea.

I venture to point out that there is another mode of approaching this subject, otherwise than through the law of conspiracy. It is quite in accordance with all precedents that every citizen should be bound to perform duties essential to the good of the State and the community. On this ground householders are compelled to serve on juries, and rich men are obliged to assume the onerous office of sheriff. Several parish offices—such as those of constable, overseer, collector of taxes, etc.—were lately obligatory, if they are not so still, obsolete or unusual though they may in many places have become. Every able-bodied man, too, is potentially a police constable, and can be fined for refusing to assist a policeman when called upon to do so. Right to the military service of all men of military age is in abeyance in this kingdom, but would, of course, be reasserted under the pressure of necessity. I presume that the *posse comitatûs* still exists in theory. But as some things become archaic, new things arise; and if our present elaborate system of trade and industry presents the chance of serious emergencies, the *posse comitatûs* should be called out in the appropriate way. In other words, there should be some legal authority capable in the last resort of obliging citizens to perform certain essential duties, whether it be the stoking of gas retorts, the mending of water conduits, or the mining of coal, essential for the life of the nation. Instead of sentencing men to penal servitude, as in former days, because they had refused to continue in their legal employment, they would be simply ordered, by competent authority, to continue to work so long as the imperative needs of society continued, ordinary compensation being given, and punishment inflicted only for breach of orders.

For this course there are, in fact, some precise legal precedents. Thus the Sewers Act (28 Henry VIII. cap. 5) gave powers to the Commissioners of Sewers to provide for the draining of the Fens, and allowed them "to arrest and take as many carts, horses, oxen, beasts, and other instruments necessary, and as many workmen and labourers as for the said works and reparation shall suffice, paying for the same competent wages, salary, and stipend." Again, the liability of parishioners and tenants personally to repair the highways by Statute Labour has only recently been commuted into money payments.

It is worthy of notice that the great railway strike in the United States, which was, in fact, an industrial insurrection, was brought to an end not by any legal process, but by the arbitrary exhibition of force. The situation having become intolerable, "a division, headed by two 12-pounder Napoleon guns and a detachment of mounted police, was marched out, supported by volunteers, to Schuler's Hall, the new headquarters of the strikers, when about ninety men were arrested without form or warrant of law, and taken off to prison. These men were subsequently examined, and discharged with cautionary counsels from the authorities" (Reports respecting the late Industrial Conflicts in the United States, 1877 [C. 1853], p. 47). In the same very instructive report we are told that about 300 discontented railway hands, and a score or two of agitators, were powerful enough to paralyse a vast system of railway traffic, and the industries of a city (St. Louis) of nearly half a million people, when "had 200 police been detailed in the first instance to compel 'hands off' the property of the railroads, and to enforce peace at all hazards, the strike would not have lasted a day."

It ought to be added that Messrs. Thomas Hughes and Frederick Harrison, the most enlightened perhaps of all the so-called "labour advocates," while condemning the policy of exceptional penalties, allow that some extraordinary danger to the public safety may justify even such an anomalous system. In their separate report under the Royal Commission of 1867, they say (Third Dissent, p. liii.)—

"It seems to us that the policy of imposing exceptional penalties upon the labouring population *en masse*, and as such recognising in that class exceptional offences, is a principle vicious in itself, and long discredited. Nothing but some extraordinary danger to the public safety, or some peculiar proneness to crime, can justify such an anomalous system. We can see nothing in the combinations of workmen which the ordinary police cannot deal with."

CHAPTER VI

CO-OPERATION AND INDUSTRIAL PARTNERSHIP

AMONG the means by which the relations of workmen and capitalists may be put on a sounder footing, much has been hoped from co-operation. The name co-operation has indeed been used in so many and such vague senses, that it has come to mean little or nothing beyond some novel form of association. Before we can say anything about it, we must distinguish at least three different classes of co-operative associations, which again in their details admit of much variety. Thus we may enumerate—

(1.) The co-operation of retail purchasers to buy their household supplies on the wholesale scale, and thus avoid the profits of the middleman.

(2.) The co-operation of workmen who form joint-stock companies for the carrying on of manufacturing or agricultural industry independently of large capitalists.

(3.) The co-operation of employers and employed in any scheme of partnership which admits the employed to a share of the ultimate profits, in addition to the wages advanced.

Of these forms of co-operation the first has little or no direct connection with the subject of this volume. There is of course not the least reason why any body of persons, whether working-men, or civil servants, or merchants, or others, may not associate themselves together to procure supplies at the lowest rates. Such associations are, or at least were, experiments, the failure of which can hardly injure any but the members. Their success, on the contrary, may lead to extensive social advantages of a kind not strictly coming within the scope of this work. The State, too, has little to do with the matter beyond allowing the utmost possible legal freedom and facilities to such associations. There is nothing whatever in the legal position or the actions of such societies, with the trifling exception of their disputed exemption from the necessity of giving receipts with penny stamps, to threaten any other industrial bodies or institutions unfairly.

Indirectly, however, co-operative associations have considerable bearing on trade questions, because they offer the most ready and engaging mode of investment for small sums of capital. Half the bitterness of trades union disputes arises from the anti-capitalist feelings of the workman, who believes that he is by the nature of things cut off from the possession of capital, and even looks upon it as contrary to the *esprit de corps* of his order to own capital. Nothing can tend more to break down this most mistaken and lamentable feeling than the insidious way in which capital accumulates in a well-managed co-operative society. Almost without knowing it, the workman finds himself a small capitalist, and when the balance has once begun visibly to grow, it is strange if the love of accumulation is not at length excited. The balance not only grows, but its growth excites the more interest because the owner, as a customer, a member, or even a committee man, assists in its growth, and may take part in the management of the affair. A savings bank deposit pays very low interest, and that interest is perfectly fixed. The depositor is entirely passive and is in respect of it a powerless dependant of the State. But savings deposited in almost any form of co-operative company tend to excite the instincts of the capitalist, and to acquaint the owner with a new view of the labour question.

It may almost go without saying that the second form of co-operative undertaking, the joint-stock association of workers, is highly desirable as far as it can be carried out. The law for so many centuries practically prohibited joint-stock enterprise that we can hardly wonder at the small progress which has yet been made in this direction among the working classes. The breakdown of the Ouseburn Co-operative Society and other hasty experiments shows that time is needful for learning the conditions of success in this direction. The Oldham Joint-Stock Mills, however, are now earning profits, and by the periodical publication of their accounts are probably preparing the way for new phases of the labour question. The law, at any rate, does not now stand in the way. The old mistaken law of unlimited liability is sufficiently set aside by the Companies Acts of 1862 and 1867, and also by the Partnership Law Amendment Act of 1865 (28 and 29 Vict. cap. 86), which allows any trader to give an employee a share of profits without thereby rendering him liable as a partner, or giving him right to demand an account. We proceed to consider the new form of industrial association which will probably emerge in time from these changes of the law.

Industrial Partnership.—It has been seen that the value of a workman's services depends not only upon his technical skill and the quantity of goods which he has helped to produce, but also upon the price at which those goods can be disposed of. Owing to unavoidable commercial fluctuations the price obtained varies from time to time in a manner defying precise anticipation. It follows that there is a large margin for loss or gain, which must fall upon the employer if the interests of the workman are to be closed by the weekly or fortnightly payment of wages. The operative, in short, is a partner who is being continually paid out of the firm, as it were, because he will not or cannot await the realisation of his labours.

There can be no doubt that the soundest possible solution of the labour question will eventually be found in such a modification of the terms of partnership as shall bind the interests of the employer and workman more closely together. Under such a system the weekly wages would be regarded merely as subsistence money or advances which the employer would make to enable the labourer and his family to await the completion of the interval between manufacture and sale. The balance of the value produced would be paid at the end of the year or half-year in the form of a dividend or bonus, consisting in a share of all surplus profits realised beyond the necessary charges of interest, wages of superintendence, cost of depreciation of capital, reserve to meet bad debts, and all other expenses of production for which the employer can fairly claim compensation. Under the name of Industrial Partnership such an arrangement has been experimentally tried in England,

and has been subject to a good deal of adverse discussion. The outlines of the scheme are familiar to all who have read with proper care John Stuart Mill's *Principles of Political Economy.*[1] I need not repeat here the details of the success attained by Leclaire, the house-decorator of Paris, in organising a partnership on this basis, including 200 employees. Nor need I do more than refer to the Paris and Orleans Railway Company, which long made a practice of distributing a bonus to its employees.

It would probably be impossible to get back to the first origin of this system. The primitive form of industrial organisation within the family, the family tribe, or the village community, was not very different. It is said that at the present day there is a system of social partnership in Hindu villages in which the division of the aggregate profits is made according to the work, ability, or capital which each individual contributes. Brentano quotes an ancient record showing that at Bruges and Ypres the masters and servants in the woollen trade divided the profits according to a fixed scale. In the herring fishery, whaling adventures, Cornish mining, and some other branches of industry, it has always been usual to make the workman's share depend partly at least upon the results. The extension of a similar system to manufacturing industry in general was until recent years practically impossible owing to the law of partnership. But it is a very remarkable fact that nearly a hundred years ago (1788), an Act was passed by the Irish Parliament to promote trade and manufacture by regulating and encouraging partnerships. It allowed

[1] Book IV. chap. vii. sect. 5. People's Edition, pp. 461-465.

persons to subscribe sums of money to men well qualified to trade, on the condition that the subscribers were not to be deemed traders on that account, or subject to any further demands.[1] Had such a law existed for a hundred years in England, it would have allowed of the growth of industrial partnership, and would in all probability have profoundly ameliorated the relations of labour and capital.

I entered into careful consideration of this subject in a lecture prepared for the Social Science Association in 1870, and published by the Society,[2] and I see no reason to alter the opinions in favour of the plan then expressed. It is true that the experimental trials of the system which were then being made by Messrs. Henry Briggs and Co. in coal mining, Messrs. Fox, Head, and Co. in iron manufacture, Mr. E. O. Greening, and others, in several branches of trade, have proved more or less unsuccessful. The industry has continued, but the partnership with the men has been given up. On the principles enunciated at the outset, to the effect that we must reason from the most direct and proximate experience available, it might seem that these failures negative the whole thing. But then, as before explained, experience requires careful interpretation; when we remember that these few experimental partnerships were started in single-handed opposition to powerful trades unions, we can see that there may have been interfering causes sufficient to ensure failure. A system like that of trades

[1] Holyoake, *History of Co-operation*, vol. ii. p. 227.

[2] On Industrial Partnerships—A Lecture delivered under the auspices of the National Association for the Promotion of Social Science. April 5, 1870. London, 1 Adam Street, Adelphi.

unionism, with all its associated ideas, has vast latent influence. When we remember that the men employed in the works in question were brought up and imbued with these ideas, we see that it must take a long time to introduce a very different system.

The present doctrine is that the workman's interests are linked to those of other workmen, and the employer's interests to those of other employers. Eventually it will be seen that industrial divisions should be perpendicular, not horizontal. The workman's interests should be bound up with those of his employer, and should be pitted in fair competition against those of other workmen and employers. There would then be no arbitrary rates of wages, no organised strikes, no long disputes rendering business uncertain and hazardous. The best workman would seek out the best master, and the best master the best workmen. Zeal to produce the best and the cheapest and most abundant goods would take the place of zeal in obstructive organisation. The faithful workman would not only receive a share of any additional profits which such zeal creates, but he would become a shareholder on a small scale in the firm, and a participator in the insurance and superannuation benefits which the firm could hold out to him with approximate certainty of solvency.

I should hesitate thus to enlarge upon the advantages of industrial partnership were they at present purely imaginary and in opposition to experience. The fact, however, is, that in France, where trades unions have never acquired much influence, the system of industrial partnership has advanced surely, and of late rapidly. Under the name of *Participation aux Bénéfices*, or participation in profit, it has been adopted by at least forty firms, many of them, such as the well-known "Bon Marché," being establishments of great extent and importance. A society, now in the third year of its existence, has been formed to study the different schemes of participation adopted, and to make them known in the Bulletin of the Society. This publication is issued by Messrs. A. Chaix et Cie., Rue Bergère, 20, Près du Boulevard Montmartre, 5 francs per volume. Payments can be made to a collector in London, who will be named on application to the secretary of the society at the address just given. Full membership of the society is obtained by payment of an annual subscription of 20 francs. The fullest details of the constitution, general management, and results of the French industrial partnerships are given in this periodical. One of the latest numbers of the Bulletin contains a complete history of the partnership accorded to its employees by the Compagnie du Chemin de Fer d'Orléans, since amalgamated with other lines. In the last year or two Mr. Sedley Taylor has drawn attention to the remarkable progress of "participation in profits" in France, and has wisely and ably advocated similar progress in this country. So great is the practical importance of the subject that I subjoin a list of the papers or books in which the reader can obtain full information :—

Charles Babbage, *Economy of Manufactures*, chap. xxvi.

H. C. Briggs, Social Science Association, 1869.

H. C. and A. Briggs, Evidence before the Trades-Union Commission, 4th March 1868. Questions 12,485 to 12,753.

The Industrial Partnerships Record.

Pare, *Co-operative Agriculture* (Longmans), 1870.

Jean Billon, *Participation des Ouvriers aux Bénéfices des Patrons*, Genève, 1877.

Fougerousse, *Patrons et Ouvriers de Paris* (Chaix), 1880.

Sedley Taylor, *Society of Arts Journal*, 18th February 1881, vol. xxix. pp. 260-70. Also in *Nineteenth Century*, May 1881, pp. 802-11, "On Profit Sharing."

To see what is being done abroad, the reader should consult *La Question Ouvrière: Essai de Solution Pratique.* Par J. C. Van Marken: Paris (Chaix), 1881.

CHAPTER VII

ARBITRATION AND CONCILIATION

HAVING regard to the failure of working-men in most cases to become their own employers by co-operation, and the apparent remoteness of the time when the system of industrial partnership is likely to be adopted in this country, we must turn with increased interest to the measures which have been taken with respect to conciliation and arbitration. A conciliator is one who intervenes between disputants in order to promote calm discussion, to draw forth frank explanations, or to suggest possible terms of compromise. The mere fact that the conciliator is, as he always ought to be, unimpassioned and disinterested, the impartial spectator of Adam Smith's theory of morals, is often sufficient to enable him to allay the irritation and to prove that the disputants are more nearly of a mind than they imagined themselves to be. An arbitrator, on the other hand, is one appointed either by the consent of the parties, or by superior authority, to inquire into the facts, to receive explanations from both sides, and then, with or without the concurrence of the disputants, to assign the terms of arrangement. The logical difference between conciliation and arbitration is that the agreement is in the former case entirely voluntary; in the latter case it is, if need be, compulsory. It follows that conciliation may be practised any day by any person, irrespective of the law or the State. To constitute arbitration in the proper sense of the term there must be some statutory or judicial power under which the arbitrators proceed. Even if the parties enter into arbitration in a perfectly voluntary way, they must surrender their freedom to a certain extent, by agreeing to accept the arbitrators' award, and thus enabling it to be judicially imposed. If this be not the case, the arbitration so called is in reality only conciliation.

It must be quite apparent, however, that the greatest possible difference exists between trade disputes according as they relate to the past, or (the present being a mere moment) to the future. When difficulties occur about the interpretation of past contracts, or questions of detail arise which were unforeseen at the time, arbitration is of course the proper and natural resource. It is the mode of settling disputes provided for in the articles of association of countless mercantile companies, in agreements of many kinds, and in the instruments of partnership of private firms. A court of law in a civil action is to a great extent a court of arbitration, but when the points of disagreement turn on questions of usage, technical practice, or complicated accounts, rather than points of law, it is usual for the judges to hand over the decision to arbitrators who are unfettered by the forms and ceremonies of the law. All such disputes relating to the past must be settled one way or the other, and when the arbitrators have been chosen and have given a decision honestly and carefully, it is proper that the result should be carried into effect compulsorily.

It is a totally different question how far agreements relating to the future conduct of trade and industry can or ought to be decided by the judgment of a third party. Here the freedom of industry is at stake, for the arbitrator will now have to decide, not what agreement was made, but what is to be made. The voluntary nature of the arrangement cannot be affected by inquiries directed merely to ascertain what the arrangement was; but in regard to the future an arbitrator in assigning the terms on which disputants are to agree necessarily restricts their liberty. The course of future events being unknown, there can be no certainty that the arbitrator knows better than the other parties. Such arbitration, then, resolves itself into the arbitrary fixing of rates of wages and prices, and other terms of working, which it is supposed, according to the principles of economics, should be left to the play of supply and demand. It is of a piece with the assize of bread and ale, and the provisions of the Statute of Apprentices which required the justices of the peace to fix rates of wages at their own discretion.

The Law of Arbitration in Labour Disputes.—Before attempting, however, to form an opinion how far some kind of conciliation or arbitration is applicable to the future, it is well to review briefly the course of legislation on the subject. Under the Elizabethan statutes there was no place for arbitration, because the conditions of labour were placed entirely in the hands of magistrates. But the decadence of that legislation was marked by the statute of the 20 Geo. II. cap. 19, which introduced a new principle by giving summary jurisdiction to justices of the peace in disputes between masters and servants when the term of hiring is one year or longer. A justice of the peace may decide all such disputes "although no rate or assessment of wages has been made that year by the justices of the peace of the shire," etc. Extensive powers were given to the magistrates for coercing refractory servants and apprentices, although there was the alternative of discharging them from their engagements. By the 31 Geo. II. cap. 11, the powers of the Act were extended to the case of agricultural servants hired for less than a year; but the magistrate's interference was clearly limited to disputes arising during the currency of a hiring, and no power was given to bind servants beyond that term.

During the eighteenth century a series of Acts was passed, partly the same as those known as the Combination Acts, which provided means for the settlement of disputes in particular trades, especially those engaged with cotton. The Act of the 43 Geo. III. (1803), cap. 151, was of a more elaborate character, and enabled disputes between masters and weavers, or such as arise with persons engaged in ornamenting cotton goods by the needle, to be settled by referees appointed by a justice of the peace. Such Acts were, however, consolidated and replaced by that of the 5 Geo. IV. cap. 96, which established one general law relating to arbitration of disputes in every branch of trade and manufacture. This Act was doubtless passed in consequence of the recommendations of the Committee of the House of Commons of 1824, which inquired into the operation of the Labour Laws. In the second section we find an enumeration of the causes of dispute which may be referred to arbitrators under the Act; but we find it carefully provided that "nothing in this Act contained shall authorise any justice or justices acting as hereinafter mentioned to establish a rate of wages or price of labour or workmanship, at which the workman shall in future be paid, unless with the mutual consent of both master and workman." There is a great contrast between the powers here given to justices and those which they enjoyed under the older laws; but it will be seen that with the consent of both parties they could settle rates prospectively. The arbitration under this Act is to be carried out by persons nominated by the justice of the peace, one half being master manufacturers and the other half workmen, out of which the master and workmen who are in dispute respectively choose one man each as referees having full power to hear and determine the dispute. In case of failure of decision other referees could be appointed, and in the last resort the justices could settle the matter finally, provided that no master manufacturer could act as justice in this capacity. This elaborate Act is in full force, only the first section having been superseded by the Statute Law Revision Act, 1873. It is, I presume, but seldom appealed to.

The Function of the Conciliator.—It is quite obvious, then, that there is ample precedent for referring trade disputes to arbitration, provided that the powers of the arbitrators shall not extend to the fixing of a future rate of wages or prices of any commodity. But, as this fixing of future rates is often the main matter in dispute, it still remains to be considered how far conciliation may apply to the future. Clearly, the consent of both the parties will be the measure of the power of the arbitrator, and, as the term of the compulsory award, if any, will be brief, prospective arbitration becomes reduced to conciliation. But the question still remains, Is there any legitimate function for a third party intervening in such disputes? Wages and prices are governed by—that is to say, manifest—the laws of supply and demand. Buyers and sellers must higgle until they hit that mean term at which business can proceed. In the corn, cotton, stock, and other large markets, no conciliators are needed to arrange quotations. The question is, Will you, or will you not buy? If one person does not buy, another does; or the price asked is shifted a little, until a buyer is attracted. Why does not the same spontaneous adjustment take place in the labour market? Probably it would take place were individual workmen and employers left alone to make separate bargains in each case. Domestic servants, for instance, arrange their terms of hiring in perfect independence; there are no strikes and no lock-outs. If an employer offers too low terms, servants are not to be had. There is the freest competition among good servants for good places, and among good employers for good servants. The general result is quite satisfactory.

The existence, however, of combinations in the labour market alters the nature of the bargains altogether. There is no longer competition among men and among employers, but we have a uniform body of men demanding a certain rate of wages, and a body of employers offering another. The laws of supply and demand do not apply to such a case. In all bargains about a single object there may arise, as I have explained in my *Theory of Political Economy* (2d ed. pp. 128-137), a dead-lock. In the sale of an estate, for instance, A may be willing to sell for £10,000, and B may in his own mind be prepared to give £11,000, if necessary. Could their minds be perfectly known to each other, any price between £10,000 and £11,000 would be possible; but there would even then be a dead-lock arising from the want of any means of determining at what point between £10,000 and £11,000 the eventual price should be fixed. As each party in a negotiation, however, conceals his own feelings and intentions as much as possible, B may believe that A will sell for £9000, and by way of dissembling his own great wish for the estate offers only £8000. The combat of desires and fears is only resolved by the lapse of time which tries the patience of both parties, unless, indeed, a third party is called in as mediator. An important negotiation of the kind is, indeed, seldom conducted by the personal meeting of the parties interested. It is handed over to their solicitors or land agents; and, when they come to a dead-lock, the independent opinion of a valuer will be appealed to, if it is obviously for the advantage of all that some bargain should be concluded.

Now, as pointed out by Mr. F. Y. Edgeworth, in his remarkable work on Mathematical Physics, the existence of combinations in trade disputes usually reduces them to a single contract bargain of the same indeterminate kind. The men, for instance, ask for 15 per cent advance of wages all round. Rather than have a strike, it might be for the interest of the employers to give the advance, or for the men to withdraw their demand; *a fortiori*, any intermediate arrangement would still more meet their views. But there may be absolutely no economic principle on which to decide the question. Mathematically speaking, the problem is an indeterminate one, and must be decided by importing new conditions.

It would appear, then, that, even on the grounds of pure economic theory, there are reasons why a conciliator might be properly called in to resolve an industrial dead-lock. Far more expedient still must this course appear when we remember that in trade disputes the economic question is often the smallest part of the matter. Masters and men belong to such different classes of society that the least difference of opinion is soon complicated with sentiments of social dislike. Ideas of so-called fairness, justice, generosity, good faith, etc., are implicated. If no mode of allaying the dispute be quickly discovered, it becomes a question of surrender or no surrender. A strike, says Mr. Newmarch, is the end of discussion and the beginning of war. As Mr. Bevan remarks, a *casus belli* no sooner arises than all prudence is thrown to the winds. Pecuniary losses are of little account to those who are prepared to endure starvation rather than submit to what they esteem "injustice." It is obvious, then, that a trade dispute, especially when it has reached the acute phase of a strike, has little or nothing to do with economics. It is not a question of science, and there is no theoretic reason why conciliators should not be called in, if experience shows that they are usually able to compose matters.

In many cases the work of such conciliators will consist in little more than inquiring into the real facts of the case, and impartially and authoritatively making them known to both parties. If either party then confesses to misapprehension, it is clear that the conciliator imports rather than ousts political economy. He acts the part of an economic and statistical inquirer. Even if a difference still exists, the conciliator may be able to suggest some medium course which it will be for the interests of both parties to accept rather than to continue a struggle ruinous to all. As in legal litigation, it is often better to have any decision rather than no decision at all. The conciliator may play the part of scapegrace, and bear the reproaches, provided only that the combatants will accept the terms and try to forget their mutual reproaches.

Results of Experience in Conciliation.—The success of the conciliation system has varied much in different trades. From a review of the facts adduced by Mr. Weeks in his valuable report upon the subject, to be presently mentioned, I should infer that success is greatest when there is a multiplicity of rates of wages and prices of work and all kinds of technical details to be settled. In the hosiery trades, for instance, this is conspicuously the case, the lists of prices and rates extending to thousands of items. In such a trade some method of arrangement must be invaluable if not indispensable, as the remarkable success attained at Nottingham by the Board originated by Mr. Mundella sufficiently shows. In many other trades the details are more numerous and perplexing than easily appears to an outsider. Thus, in the building trades generally there are not only the principal rates of wages to be paid, but the rates for overtime, the time of payment, the length of notice, the hours of beginning and ending work, and the intervals allowed for meals. The allowance of "walking time," or the time required for getting to and from the place of work, is also a fruitful cause of dispute. When all such matters are arranged to the satisfaction of both parties, there arises a complete code of working rules, like that prepared by Mr. Davis for the bricklayers and builders of the Staffordshire potteries. Such troublesome details must be settled by custom or by some kind of rule, written or unwritten. The laws of supply and demand cannot settle such details. And if disputes and strikes are shown by experience to be fewest under a system of arbitration, it is difficult to deny the utility of the system.

Much less success has so far attended the practice of arbitration in the great branches of mining industry and metallurgy. When a single decision affects in a serious degree the interests of a very large body of men, or a very large mass of capital, it is difficult to induce the parties to submit so important a matter to the judgment of a single mind. The employers affirm that they cannot yield demands for higher wages without suffering a large pecuniary loss. Nothing but necessity, then, can make them yield. The men, on the other hand, will not be satisfied by the assurances of the most respectable arbitrator. Thus either the dead-lock is maintained without arbitration, or the awards of arbitrators are unfortunately repudiated in some cases by the men, or in rare cases by the masters. It is to be hoped, however, that arbitration may make progress even among colliers; there must be many matters relating to modes of weighing, safety of mines, convenience of labour, etc., which might be settled by a board, and an approach to a better understanding about wages should be made through a sliding scale. In several cases, indeed, sliding scale agreements have recently broken down, and the experience of arbitration in the great trades alluded to is rather discouraging. But in the absence of any better method of composing strife, the only course seems to be to try again and again, until the parties learn the superior advantages of industrial peace. It must be obvious, however, that both the sliding scale and the system of arbitration generally should be regarded as no permanent settlement of the relations of workmen and employers, but rather as a stepping-stone to some still sounder method of partnership and participation in profits which a future generation will certainly enjoy.

A very careful and impartial inquiry into the methods and success of arbitration and conciliation in this country was made a few years ago by Mr. Jos. D. Weeks, special commissioner of the State of Pennsylvania. It is entitled, "Report on the Practical Operation of Arbitration and Conciliation in the Settlement of Differences between Employers and Employees in England. . . . Harrisburg (U.S.A.), 1879." It is probably the most valuable document published on the subject, describing both the successes and failures of the system.[1] Reference should also be made to Mr. Rupert Kettle's valuable evidence before the Trades-Union Commissioners of 1867 (Questions 6985 to 7231), and to Mr. Henry Crompton's well-known "Essay on Industrial Conciliation."

Conseils de Prud'hommes.—The comparatively brief experience furnished by boards of arbitration in this

[1] See also Mr. Weeks' later report on Industrial Conciliation and Arbitration in New York, Ohio, and Pennsylvania, in the Twelfth Annual Report of the *Massachusetts Bureau of Statistics of Labor.* Boston, 1881.

country is fortified by the long and successful action of somewhat similar bodies in France and Belgium. Though invested with judicial power, and placed upon a legal footing, the Conseils de Prud'hommes are in part of their functions closely analogous to the volunteer conciliators of the English manufacturing districts. The name *prud'hommes* (wise men) carries us back to the mediæval *communautés* or guilds of arts and trades in France. They were the experts chosen to judge the soundness of commodities or to settle trifling disputes between merchants and manufacturers at fairs. The Revolution made an end of all such antiquated institutions, so far as they had not already fallen into disuse; but it is curious to find that the eleventh year of the Republic had not elapsed before the City of Lyons discovered the necessity of some kind of trade tribunal, and the law of the 21 Germinal of that year, although applying at first only to Lyons, soon became the basis on which similar *conseils* were established in many other French towns. The members of the *conseil* are elected by all the employers, managers, foremen, and workmen of the industries coming under its purview, the *maire* of the *commune* preparing the voting lists, and the *prefet* acting as returning officer. The masters and men are convoked separately, and return to the council equal numbers of their own body. The president and vice-president are nominated by the chief of the executive power (*i.e.* the Central Government), and the council thus constituted retains its power for three years. It is divided into two *bureaux* or committees—the *bureau général*, composed of at least five members, meeting once a week, and the *bureau particulier*, consisting of one master and one workman, who attend every day for two hours. All disputants are "invited," in the first place, to come before the *bureau particulier*, in order to "explain" their differences. If this result be not achieved, they are summoned more formally before the *bureau général*, which disposes authoritatively of the matter, if falling within their competence. It is plain that the *bureau particulier* represents conciliation as contrasted with the arbitration of the *bureau général*.

From Mr. Bevan's paper on Strikes (*Journal of the Statistical Society*, March 1880, vol. xliii. pp. 35-64) we learn that the numbers of cases brought before these bodies annually in France have varied from 30,000 up to 45,000. In about 70 per cent of the cases conciliation was sufficient, while a considerable number of cases were eventually settled outside the court. Of the causes of dispute, 61 per cent related to wages, 14 per cent to dismissals, and 5 per cent to apprenticeship cases. The *conseils* also have cognisance of property in designs, trade-marks, and some other matters not coming within our present subject.

A considerable body of law has grown up in France around these tribunals, the functions of which are carefully defined and regulated. Those who are interested in the subject can learn the whole constitution, law, and practice from any of several admirable little manuals which have been drawn up by French advocates. It will be sufficient to mention the *Code Pratique des Prud'hommes*, par Th. Sarrazin, 3e ed. 2e Tirage, Paris, 1880 (Marchal, Billard, et Cie. Prix 1 franc 50 cent.)

The Best Constitution of Boards of Conciliation.—The

question still remains how far Boards of Arbitration and Conciliation in this country ought to be connected with or regulated by the State. The long-continued success of the Conseils de Prud'hommes, which are distinctly State tribunals, would lead us to expect good results from a like institution here. But the analogy between French and English institutions is never a very safe ground of inference, and experience in England tends rather to show that the more the arbitrating bodies originate in the voluntary action of the parties concerned, the more they are likely to carry weight. An attempt has, indeed, been made to give a legal basis to such bodies, by the passing of the 30 and 31 Vict. cap. 105 (1867), entitled, "An Act to establish Equitable Councils of Conciliation to adjust differences between masters and workmen." After reciting, without repealing, three of the previous Acts already mentioned (p. 151) relating to arbitration, this new Act gives power to Her Majesty, or the Secretary of State for the Home Department, to grant a license for the formation of a council, after receiving a joint petition from any number of persons, who as masters shall have resided in a place for six months, or as workmen shall have so resided six months, and shall also have worked at the trade for seven years previous to the signing of the petition. The petitioners shall, at a meeting specially convened for the purpose, agree to form a council, and notice of the intention must be published, one month before the application, in the London *Gazette*, and in one or more newspapers of the locality. The masters and men of two or more adjoining boroughs or districts of the metropolis may associate themselves together in these matters. The council is to consist of not less than two, nor more than ten, masters and workmen, together with a chairman; but no member can adjudicate in a cause in which he or any of his relatives is concerned. The petitioners are to elect the first council, which, after appointing their chairman, clerk, and other requisite officers, shall have power to hear and determine all differences between masters and workmen, as set forth in the Act of the 5 Geo. IV. cap. 96, which may be submitted to them by both parties. The award is to be final and conclusive, and may be enforced by proceedings of distress, sale, or imprisonment, as provided in the recited Acts. It is, however, specially provided that "nothing in this Act contained shall authorise the said council to establish a rate of wages, or price of labour, or workmanship, at which the workman shall in future be paid." The quorum of the council is to consist of three members, but a committee called the Committee of Conciliation, appointed by the council, and consisting of one master and one workman, shall endeavour to reconcile all differences in the first instance. The chairman is to be unconnected with trade, and has a casting voice. No counsel, solicitors, or attorneys are to be heard before the council or committee without the consent of both parties. The council is to be elected annually on the 1st November, and any inhabitant householder, who as a master has resided six months, or as a man has resided for a like period, and worked for seven years at the trade, is entitled to be registered as a voter. The proceedings at the election are carefully prescribed, and a schedule gives the various official forms required, including warrants of distress and commitment.

Evidently these Equitable Councils of Conciliation are imitations of the French Conseils de Prud'hommes, with some infusion of the older English law of arbitration. They are courts of law in disguise, and although care is taken to make them as impartial as possible, it is to be doubted, and experience confirms the doubt, whether they will meet with any favour. As such legally constituted councils are very properly prohibited from fixing rates of wages for the future, they fail to give aid just where aid is needed. All available evidence tends to show that successful boards of conciliation must be purely volunteer bodies, with no taint of the justice of the peace about them, and no powers of distress and commitment.

In all probability success will best be obtained in the settlement of trade disputes by keeping lawyers and laws as much at a distance as possible. There must be spontaneous or at least voluntary approximation of the parties concerned. It is a question not of litigation, but of shaking hands in a friendly manner, and sitting down to a table to talk the matter over. The great evil of the present day is the entire disunion of the labourer and the capitalist; if we once get the hostile bodies to meet by delegates round the same table on a purely voluntary and equal footing, the first great evil of disunion is in a fair way of being overcome. There might arise danger of joint conspiracy against the outside public, but on the whole the evils thus likely to arise are less considerable than those connected with strikes.

CHAPTER VIII

CONCLUDING REMARKS

ON reviewing the arguments given in the little treatise now brought to a close, it may perhaps seem to the reader that the results obtained are hesitating and conflicting, if not positively contradictory. We started with the task of determining in what cases the State should or should not interfere with industrial freedom.

Ancient restrictive legislation such as that of the Statute of Apprentices was denounced; and even the slight modern remnant, the practice of apprenticing youths for seven years, was described as slavery; the common law doctrine of non-restraint of trade was held up as wise in the highest degree; yet at the same time the modern Factory Acts were treated as admirable, and additional restrictions were advocated in the cases of mothers-of-young-children employed in factories, shop-assistants, and some other cases.

Anything approaching to a government superintendence of industry or official inspection of commodities was treated as out of the question; yet certain branches of trade, it was concluded, could be advantageously regulated by government.

Passing to another branch of the subject, the interference of trade societies in productive industry was, as a general rule, deprecated; yet the existence and proceedings of certain professional unions and newly-created institutes of various sorts were defended. Though it was held that trades unions ought not to settle the course of trade, yet it was argued that courts of conciliation, if not of arbitration, might decide many matters which, according to the pure principles of political economy, ought to be left to the action of the laws of supply and demand.

All this savours of paradox and contradiction, but only on a superficial view of the matter. The subject is one in which we need above all things—discrimination. Restrictions on industry are not good nor bad *per se*, but according as they are imposed wisely and with good intentions, or foolishly, and with sinister intentions. *Primâ facie*, indeed, restriction is bad, because Providence is wiser than the legislator—that is to say, the action of the natural forces of evolution will ensure welfare better than the ill-considered laws of the prejudiced and unskilful legislator. But reason is a Divine gift, and where upon the grounds of clear experience interpreted by logical reasoning we can see our way to a definite improvement in some class of people without injuring others, we are under the obligation of endeavouring to promote that improvement. The greater part of the interference of trade societies is objectionable, because, though directed toward the welfare of a part, it is directed against the welfare of the rest of the community. All other industrial problems must be solved by similar careful estimation of the total utilitarian results.

If such be a true view of the case it is clear that there can be no royal road to legislation in such matters. We cannot expect to agree in utilitarian estimates, at least without much debate. We must agree to differ, and though we are bound to argue fearlessly, it should be with the consciousness that there is room for wide and *bonâ fide* difference of opinion. We must consent to advance cautiously, step by step, feeling our way, adopting no foregone conclusions, trusting no single science, expecting no infallible guide. We must neither maximise the functions of government at the beck of quasi-military officials, nor minimise them according to the theories of the very best philosophers. We must learn to judge each case upon its merits, interpreting with painful care all experience which can be brought to bear upon the matter.

Moreover, we must remember that, do what we will, we are not to expect approach to perfection in social affairs. We must recognise the fact clearly that we have to deal with complex aggregates of people and institutions, which we cannot usually dissect and treat piecemeal. We must often take "all in all or not at all." Tolerance therefore is indispensable. We may be obliged to bear with evil for a time that we may avoid a worse evil, or that we may not extinguish the beginnings of good. In the end we shall not be disappointed if our efforts are really directed towards that good of the people which was long ago pronounced to be the highest law.

THE END

www.ingramcontent.com/pod-product-compliance
Ingram Content Group UK Ltd.
Pitfield, Milton Keynes, MK11 3LW, UK
UKHW021959180926
475701UK00003B/95
* 9 7 8 0 7 6 5 8 0 8 6 7 7 *